I0099850

International Regulatory Co-operation

OECD

BETTER POLICIES FOR BETTER LIVES

This document, as well as any data and map included herein, are without prejudice to the status of or sovereignty over any territory, to the delimitation of international frontiers and boundaries and to the name of any territory, city or area.

Please cite this publication as:
OECD (2021), *International Regulatory Co-operation*, OECD Best Practice Principles for Regulatory Policy, OECD Publishing, Paris, *https://doi.org/10.1787/5b28b589-en*.

ISBN 978-92-64-57839-5 (print)
ISBN 978-92-64-79132-9 (pdf)

OECD Best Practice Principles for Regulatory Policy
ISSN 2311-6005 (print)
ISSN 2311-6013 (online)

Preface

The 2008 financial crisis and the COVID-19 pandemic have exposed the interdependence and complexity of today's world. Addressing both crises required unprecedented multilateral co-operation efforts. Similarly, many of the challenges we face, climate and biodiversity change, transboundary pollution, tax evasion and avoidance, digitalisation, financial market instability, or migration flows, cannot be dealt with by domestic governments alone. These challenges and many others can only be addressed effectively with international regulatory co-operation across all relevant policy fronts. Even so, we continue to witness how institutional frameworks and regulatory processes are too constrained by traditional jurisdictional boundaries and, as such, fail to recognise the global scope of the issues that they need to address.

That's why governments need to adjust their approach to rulemaking. They need to consider the international realities when developing their domestic laws and regulations. By applying a stronger, more systematic international lens in their rulemaking practices, governments will be better equipped to learn from each other and, when needed, articulate co-ordinated and consistent regulatory responses while preserving their national prerogatives. There are many impressive examples of the benefits of regulatory cooperation – from the number of lives saved through regulators working together on vaccine approval, to the coordination of air transport health safety protocols during the pandemic, the improvement of air or water quality resulting from coordination in pollution standards, the security offered to consumers by enforcement beyond borders, and the large financial benefits for traders and investors from limiting the unnecessary divergence in product requirements.

The OECD Best Practice Principles on International Regulatory Co-operation report lays down the key principles and priority approaches on *how* rulemaking procedures can be fundamentally transformed to strengthen resilience to the disruptions of an interconnected world economy. These principles aim to support governments in making a more effective and strategic use of different co-operation alternatives, including international instruments.

It was visionary when the OECD Regulatory Policy Committee made international regulatory co-operation a pillar of regulatory quality in 2012. It is no coincidence that these Best Practice Principles – the first and only guide on the topic at the international level, drawing on nearly 10 years of policy research and analysis in the field – are launched when the OECD is promoting global cooperation as key to optimising the strength and the quality of the economic recovery in the wake of COVID-19 and address other pressing global challenges. The Best Practice Principles confirm the Organisation's dedication to supporting governments in harnessing all facets of globalisation, managing the global commons and promoting multilateralism to achieve ambitious global commitments such as the Sustainable Development Goals. The development of these Best Practice Principles on International Regulatory Co-operation is a key milestone and I invite all countries to actively use them to make governments more aware of the transboundary reach of their actions, and design better policies for better lives.

Mathias Cormann

OECD Secretary-General

Foreword

This report is part of the series of "best practice principles" produced under the auspices of the OECD Regulatory Policy Committee.

Established domestic regulatory mechanisms and tools are reaching their limits to cope with transboundary challenges. The rapid internationalisation of markets, goods, flows, as well as common threats such as the COVID-19 pandemic presents unprecedented challenges to policy makers and regulators that cannot be dealt with in isolation. There is an urgent need for more consistent, resilient and dynamic rules to face the increasing complexity of issues. International regulatory co-operation (IRC) provides an opportunity for countries to consider the impacts of their regulations beyond their borders, expand the evidence basis for decision making learning from the experience of their international peers, and develop concerted approaches to challenges that transcend borders. As part of custom regulatory activities, IRC can strengthen the competence of public administrations on global issues.

The OECD Regulatory Policy Committee (RPC) has played a leading international role in promoting regulatory reform and sound regulatory practices across the whole of government. It identified the importance of IRC as early as 1994 and systematically collected a profound acquis on analytical work from 2011. Pursuant to the visionary Principle 12 of the 2012 Recommendation on Regulatory Policy and Governance [OECD/LEGAL/0309], which encourages Adherents to "*give consideration to all relevant international standards and frameworks for co-operation in the same field and, where appropriate, their likely effects on parties outside the jurisdiction*", RPC work has taken several directions. It has stabilised the definitions and key concepts around IRC; investigating the various IRC approaches through a range of studies of specific sectors (i.e. financial sector), policy areas (i.e. competition) or approaches (i.e. mutual recognition); unpacking the interface between regulatory and trade policy; highlighting the contribution of international organisations; analysing the national levers for embedding IRC in domestic rulemaking; and led to the development of dedicated IRC platforms (such as the Partnership of International Organisations for Effective International Rulemaking). With the Best Practice Principles on International Regulatory Co-operation ("Best Practice Principles"), the RPC builds on and synthesises this work and consolidates its role as the only international forum with recognised expertise on regulatory policy and with a well-established normative basis on IRC.

The Best Practice Principles intend to assist policymakers and civil servants with practical guidance to make better use of IRC. They outline essential steps in defining a whole of government strategy and governance, to embed international considerations throughout the regulatory design, development and delivery, and to leverage bilateral, regional and multilateral co-operation on regulatory matters to support national policy objectives.

The Best Practice Principles bring together expertise from a broad range of stakeholders. Beyond leveraging the wealth of knowledge of the OECD RPC members, a public consultation conducted in January – March 2021 led to valuable inputs from governments, international organisations, civil society, and different OECD policy communities.

This document was approved by the Regulatory Policy Committee at its 24th Session on 21st April 2021 and prepared for publication by the OECD Secretariat.

Acknowledgements

The Best Practice Principles on International Regulatory Co-operation were prepared by the OECD Public Governance Directorate (GOV) under the leadership of Elsa Pilichowski, Public Governance Director and Nick Malyshev, Head of the Regulatory Policy Division. They were drafted and managed by Céline Kauffmann in co-ordination with Marianna Karttunen and Camila Saffirio. Thanks are extended to staff of the OECD Regulatory Policy Division who provided inputs throughout the development of the document. The editorial process was co-ordinated by Jennifer Stein.

The authors are especially grateful for substantial discussions and invaluable insights from the members of the Steering Group on International Regulatory Co-operation (comprised as of 2021 of Australia, Canada, Chile, Colombia, the European Commission, Germany, Mexico, New Zealand, Norway, the United Kingdom and the United States).

The Secretariat pays particular thanks to members of the Regulatory Policy Committee who provided substantial comments and support to the various drafts of the document, particularly in April and October/November 2020, as well as members of the Network of Economic Regulators for their inputs. In addition, the document benefitted greatly from extensive inputs received throughout a public consultation conducted in January – March 2021, particularly from representatives of governments, international bodies, civil society as well as other OECD policy communities.

Table of contents

Tables

Figures

Boxes

Abbreviations and acronyms

ACER	Agency for the Co-operation of Energy Regulators
AI	Artificial Intelligence
APEC	Asia-Pacific Economic Cooperation
BCBS	Basle Committee on Banking Supervision
BEPS	Base Erosion and Profit Shifting
BPPs	Best Practice Principles
BIAC	Businesses at OECD
CABs	Conformity assessment bodies
CCRVDF	Codex Committee on Residues of Veterinary Drugs in Foods
CDR	Cabinet Directive on Regulation
CETA	EU-Canada Comprehensive Economic and Trade Agreement
CFR	Community of Federal Regulators
CLRTAP	Convention on Long-range Transboundary Air Pollution
EC	European Commission
EMA	European Medicines Agency
EU	European Union
FAO	Food and Agriculture Organisation
FSB	Financial Stability Board
FTA	Free Trade Agreement
GEMS	Greenhouse and Energy Minimum Standards
G-REG	Government Regulatory Practice Initiative
GRP	Good Regulatory Practices
IAIS	International Association of Insurance Supervisors
IASB	International Accounting Standards Board
ICN	International Competition Network
IFAC	International Federation of Accountants
IGA	Intergovernmental agreement
IGO	Intergovernmental organisation
IO	International organisation
IOSCO	International Organization of Securities Commissions

IPPC	International Plant Protection Convention
IRC	International regulatory co-operation
ITF	International Transport Forum
MAD	Mutual Acceptance of Data
MLAT	Mutual Legal Assistance Treaty
MLI	Multilateral Convention to Implement Tax Treaty Related Measures to Prevent BEPS
MoU	Memorandum of Understanding
MRA	Mutual Recognition Agreement
MBIE	Ministry of Business, Innovation and of Foreign Employment
NIOSH	National Institute for Occupational Safety and Health
NTM	Non-tariff measures
OMB	Office of Management and Budget
OECD	Organisation for Economic Co-operation and Development
OIE	World Organisation for Animal Health
RCC	Canada-US Regulatory Cooperation Council
RCF	Regulatory Cooperation Forum
RIA	Regulatory impact assessment
RPC	Regulatory Policy Committee
RTA	Regional trade agreement
SPS	Sanitary and phytosanitary
TBS	Treasury Board Secretariat of Canada
TBT	Technical barriers to trade
TGN	Trans-governmental network
UNECE	United Nations Commission for Europe
USMCA	United Stated-Mexico-Canada Agreement
US FDA	United States Food and Drug Administration
VICH	International Cooperation on Harmonisation of Technical Requirements of Veterinary Medicinal Products
WAHIS	World Animal Health Information System
WHO	World Health Organization
WTO	World Trade Organization

Executive summary

Rapid transboundary flows of goods and services, particularly leveraged by the dematerialisation brought by digitalisation, are testing the effectiveness and the capacity of domestic regulatory frameworks. At the same time, the increasing economic interdependency may also have made the world more vulnerable to common threats, particularly visible in times of global crisis. Climate change, financial market instabilities, tax evasion and avoidance, and most recently, the COVID-19 pandemic are just a few examples of complex global challenges whose public management revealed shortcomings in the international coordination of regulation. They are a stark reminder of the interconnectedness of countries and the importance of co-operation in laws and regulations to improve the resilience of regulatory frameworks in the face of global or regional disruptions.

International Regulatory Co-operation (IRC) aims to promote the interoperability of legal and regulatory frameworks. The 2012 OECD Recommendation on Regulatory Policy and Governance was visionary in making IRC a key pillar of the quality and relevance of regulation by encouraging governments, in developing regulatory measures, to *give consideration to all relevant international standards and frameworks for co-operation in the same field and, where appropriate, their likely effects on parties outside the jurisdiction* (Principle 12). IRC thus forms part of a critical building block of structural regulatory reform, bridging the gap between the domestic nature of rulemaking and the increasingly international dimension of issues that laws and regulations aim to address. The OECD Best Practice Principle on International Regulatory Co-operation ("Best Practice Principles") provide policy makers, civil servants and other public sector practitioners with a practical instrument to make the best of IRC.

There are various ways in which government authorities can promote the interoperability of laws and regulations. Broadly, the notion of IRC encompasses any agreement or organisational arrangement, formal or informal, between countries to promote some form of co-operation in the design, monitoring, enforcement, or ex-port management of regulation. In practice, IRC approaches range from the exchange of information to the harmonisation of rules. They may focus on the stage preceding the development of rules – such as the evidence gathering – or apply to the regulatory delivery side (in enforcement/inspection for example). They may involve complex institutional organisation (such as the establishment of a dedicated secretariat) or result from informal dialogue. To draw benefits from IRC, it is essential for policymakers and regulators to consider the broad range of approaches and their respective benefits and costs.

To support countries in operating a true culture shift and firmly embed a stronger international lens in domestic regulatory frameworks, the Best Practice Principles are organised around three building blocks (and detailed below).

Establishing a whole-of-government IRC policy/strategy is an essential step to convey political leadership and build a holistic vision, feeding into the broader strategic priorities of the government, with clearly defined roles and responsibilities. More broadly, it helps the diversity of actors that need to be involved in IRC in having common understanding and awareness of the tools available to them.

IRC starts at home with embedding its key principles throughout the domestic rulemaking, from the initiation of new laws and regulations to their implementation, evaluation and revision. This can be done without prior co-ordination with foreign peers, but still has important implications for the activities of domestic regulators and their oversight bodies. It involves a systematic consideration of foreign and international regulatory frameworks of relevance when regulating, as well as the assessment of how regulatory measures impact and fit within the broader cross-border management of the issue to address. The regulatory management tools, namely regulatory impact assessment, stakeholder engagement and *ex post* reviews of laws and regulation, provide important entry points in the rule-making process to consider the international environment and enrich the evidence basis for the development and revision of quality laws and regulations. Ultimately better informed rulemaking helps avoid the unnecessary regulatory divergences and foster the mutual knowledge and confidence needed across jurisdictions.

In addition to unilateral actions, stronger forms of bilateral, regional or international co-operation approaches are needed (and de facto exist) to lay the ground of institutionalised and continuous collaboration and of greater coherence in regulatory matters. The modalities of co-operation will depend on the legal and administrative system and geographic location of the country, as well as on the sector or policy area under consideration. These Best Practice Principles support countries in making more effective and strategic use of such different co-operation means, such as contributing to international fora, which support regulatory co-operation, using mutual recognition in combination with other international instruments, or specific provisions in trade agreements.

These Best Practice Principles are intentionally ambitious. To date, few countries meet the principles laid down in this document. Nevertheless, because it is scarcely used does not mean that IRC is not achievable. On the contrary, a number of practices and approaches are easy to adopt. Close to 10 years after the *2012 OECD Recommendation on Regulatory Policy and Governance* made IRC a key pillar of regulatory quality, these Best Practice Principles give a renewed impetus to countries to truly embrace IRC and thus address better the major policy challenges of today and tomorrow.

Best Practice Principles on IRC

Establishing the IRC strategy and its governance

- Develop a whole of government IRC policy / strategy
- Establish a co-ordination mechanism in government on IRC activities to centralise relevant information on IRC practices and activities and to build a consensus and common language
- Enable an IRC conducive framework – i.e. raise awareness of IRC, build on existing platforms for co-operation, reduce anti-IRC biases and build in incentives for policy makers and regulators

Embedding IRC throughout the domestic rulemaking

- Gather and rely on international knowledge and expertise
- Consider existing international instruments when developing regulation and document the rationale for departing from them
- Assess impacts beyond borders
- Engage actively with foreign stakeholders
- Embed consistency with international instruments as a key principle driving the review process in *ex post* evaluation and stock reviews
- Assess *ex ante* the co-operation needs to ensure appropriate enforcement and streamline "recognisable" procedures

---

Co-operating internationally (bilaterally, plurilaterally & multilaterally)

- Co-operate with other countries to promote the development and diffusion of good practices and innovations in regulatory policy and governance
- Contribute to international fora which support regulatory co-operation
- Use mutual recognition in combination with international instruments
- Align IRC expectations across various policy instruments, including in trade agreements

Background and context

International Regulatory Co-operation (IRC) is about promoting the interoperability of legal and regulatory frameworks. Global crisis are a stark reminder of the importance of having in place effective systems of IRC. The financial crisis of 2008 revealed some of the shortcomings in the international co-ordination of financial regulation and their consequences for global financial stability. Different IRC initiatives emerged in its aftermaths, for example with regard to the prudential regulation and supervision of banks at the global level (OECD, 2013[1]) or the *OECD Policy Framework for Effective and Efficient Financial Regulation*, which was particularly important in helping regulatory convergence in the post-Global Financial Crisis era. (OECD, 2010[2]). More recently, the COVID-19 crisis has reinforced the importance of IRC as a critical building block of regulatory policy. It has illustrated the need for greater co-ordination of laws and regulations to support the availability across borders of essentials such as medical and food, to promote work sharing, mutual learning and pooling of resources between governments to adapt their responses to the crisis and to improve the resilience of regulatory frameworks in the face of disruption.

The *OECD Best Practice Principles on International Regulatory Co-operation* (the Best Practice Principles), aim to support the implementation of the *2012 OECD Recommendation on Regulatory and Policy Governance* [OECD/LEGAL/0390] (the 2012 Recommendation), which encourages Members and non-Members having adhered to it (hereafter Adherents) to *"give consideration to all relevant international standards and frameworks for co-operation in the same field and, where appropriate, their likely effects on parties outside the jurisdiction"* (Principle 12). As such, the Best Practice Principles provide policy-makers and civil servants in Adherents with practical guidance to make better use of IRC.

The Best Practice Principles aim to continue the series of reports on best practice principles for regulatory policy produced under the auspices of the OECD Regulatory Policy Committee (RPC), which provides further guidance and elaboration on the principles embodied in the 2012 Recommendation (OECD, 2012[3]).[1]

This document builds on and synthesises OECD work on IRC carried out since 2011 (Box 1). The RPC work on this has taken several directions, including stabilising the definitions and key concepts around IRC; investigating the various IRC approaches through a range of studies of specific sectors (i.e. financial sector), policy areas (i.e. competition) or approaches (i.e. mutual recognition); unpacking the interface between regulatory and trade policy; highlighting the contribution of international organisations; and analysing the national levers for embedding IRC in domestic rulemaking.

The Best Practice Principles provide a list of elements or building blocks to advance and strengthen international regulatory co-operation efforts which may be used by interested governments. They aim to be adapted to the variety of legal systems and administrative cultures among the OECD and partner countries. They can inform individual governments, leaving a sufficient degree of flexibility for administrations to adapt those policies according to local conditions. They may also provide a useful reference for governments' practical guidance and capacity building initiatives. They are accompanied by the development of other tools, such as the (APEC-OECD, Forthcoming[4]) that aims to provide a databank of case studies of IRC and a *Compendium of IO Practices* (OECD, Forthcoming[5]).

Box 1. OECD Regulatory Policy Committee work on international regulatory co-operation

The backbone of the OECD Regulatory Policy Committee work on IRC is the 2012 Recommendation, which is aimed at building and strengthening capacity for regulatory quality and reform. To support Adherents in implementing Principle 12 of the Recommendation, the OECD Regulatory Policy Committee has conducted in-depth analytical work to clarify the scope, benefits and challenges of IRC. In this sense, (OECD, 2013[6]) started by setting a working definition of IRC and establishing a typology of the different ways in which a country may approach regulatory co-operation. The typology differentiates 11 IRC approaches, from the most constraining (seldom harmonisation through joint institutions) to the lightest form of co-operation (exchange of information). The RPC went further and defined the range of benefits and costs/challenges to be expected from the various identified forms of IRC (OECD, 2013[6]) (OECD, 2017[7]).

Subsequent documents have gone in depth into mapping the respective costs and benefits by form of IRC, including of mutual recognition arrangements (Correia de Brito, Kauffmann and Pelkmans, 2016[8]), the contribution of good regulatory practices (Kauffmann and Basedow, 2016[9]), the role of international organisations (OECD, 2016[10]) and of trans-governmental networks of regulators (Abbott, Kauffmann and Lee, 2018[11]), and exploring the specific interface between IRC and trade policy (OECD, 2017[7]). This clarification of IRC has been accompanied by illustrative case studies in different thematic areas (Kauffmann and Saffirio, 2020[12]) (OECD, 2013[13]) (OECD, 2013[1]) (OECD, 2013[14]).

Following (OECD, 2013[6]) RPC work on IRC has focused on two key pillars: exploring the insertion of international considerations in domestic rulemaking and understanding the contribution of international rulemaking to IRC. The first pillar has involved identifying the key practices that policy makers may adopt at domestic level to systematise IRC. This was explored by embedding relevant questions in the survey of Regulatory Policy and Governance and reflected in the 2018 *Regulatory Policy Outlook* (OECD, 2018[15]), as well as through the conduct of in-depth country reviews of Mexico (OECD, 2018[15]) and of the UK (OECD, 2020[16]). This work has highlighted the importance of developing a common language and catalysing the efforts of different policy communities to foster IRC, including of regulatory oversight, various sectoral portfolio and trade policy makers.

The second pillar has involved investigating the role played by international organisations, as defined for the current document, as platforms for international regulatory co-operation (OECD, 2016[10]) (OECD, 2019[17]), a domain where to date little structured comparative information exists. Consequently, a Partnership of International Organisations for Effective International Rulemaking was established in 2014 to provide a framework for exchange of practices, data collection and analytical work on the effectiveness of international rulemaking. The work has sought to analyse the practices of international organisations in the development of international instruments that are in turn used at national level and the respective role of the IOs, their members and secretariats, in ensuring the quality of such instruments.

Source: http://www.oecd.org/gov/regulatory-policy/irc.htm.

Note

[1] To date the series includes guidance on One-Stop Shops for Citizens and Business (2020), Regulatory Impact Assessment (RIA), Regulatory Enforcement and Inspections Toolkit (2018), The Governance of Regulators (2014) and Regulatory Enforcement and Inspections (2014).

References

Abbott, K., C. Kauffmann and J. Lee (2018), "The contribution of trans-governmental networks of regulators to international regulatory co-operation", *OECD Regulatory Policy Working Papers*, No. 10, OECD Publishing, Paris, https://dx.doi.org/10.1787/538ff99b-en. [11]

APEC-OECD (Forthcoming), *APEC-OECD IRC Resource*. [4]

Correia de Brito, A., C. Kauffmann and J. Pelkmans (2016), "The contribution of mutual recognition to international regulatory co-operation", *OECD Regulatory Policy Working Papers*, No. 2, OECD Publishing, Paris, https://dx.doi.org/10.1787/5jm56fqsfxmx-en. [8]

Kauffmann, C. and R. Basedow (2016), "The political economy of international co-operation – a theoretical framework to understand international regulatory co-operation (IRC)", OECD, Paris, unpublished working paper. [9]

Kauffmann, C. and C. Saffirio (2020), "Study of International Regulatory Co-operation (IRC) arrangements for air quality: The cases of the Convention on Long-Range Transboundary Air Pollution, the Canada-United States Air Quality Agreement, and co-operation in North East Asia", *OECD Regulatory Policy Working Papers*, No. 12, OECD Publishing, Paris, https://dx.doi.org/10.1787/dc34d5e3-en. [12]

OECD (2020), *Review of International Regulatory Co-operation of the United Kingdom*, OECD Publishing, Paris, https://dx.doi.org/10.1787/09be52f0-en. [16]

OECD (2019), *The Contribution of International Organisations to a Rule-Based International System: Key Results from the Partnership of International Organisations for Effective Rulemaking*, https://www.oecd.org/gov/regulatory-policy/IO-Rule-Based%20System.pdf. [17]

OECD (2018), *OECD Regulatory Policy Outlook 2018*, OECD Publishing, Paris, https://dx.doi.org/10.1787/9789264303072-en. [15]

OECD (2017), *International Regulatory Co-operation and Trade: Understanding the Trade Costs of Regulatory Divergence and the Remedies*, OECD Publishing, Paris, https://dx.doi.org/10.1787/9789264275942-en. [7]

OECD (2016), *International Regulatory Co-operation: The Role of International Organisations in Fostering Better Rules of Globalisation*, OECD Publishing, Paris, https://dx.doi.org/10.1787/9789264244047-en. [10]

OECD (2013), *International Regulatory Co-operation: Case Studies, Vol. 1: Chemicals, Consumer Products, Tax and Competition*, OECD Publishing, Paris, https://dx.doi.org/10.1787/9789264200487-en. [13]

OECD (2013), *International Regulatory Co-operation: Case Studies, Vol. 2: Canada-US Co-operation, EU Energy Regulation, Risk Assessment and Banking Supervision*, OECD Publishing, Paris, https://dx.doi.org/10.1787/9789264200500-en. [1]

OECD (2013), *International Regulatory Co-operation: Case Studies, Vol. 3: Transnational Private Regulation and Water Management*, OECD Publishing, Paris, https://dx.doi.org/10.1787/9789264200524-en. [14]

16 |

OECD (2013), *International Regulatory Co-operation: Addressing Global Challenges*, OECD   [6]
    Publishing, Paris, https://dx.doi.org/10.1787/9789264200463-en.

OECD (2012), *Recommendation of the Council on Regulatory Policy and Governance*,   [3]
    http://www.oecd.org/gov/regulatory-policy/2012-recommendation.htm (accessed on
    14 March 2019).

OECD (2010), *Policy Framework for Effective and Efficient Financial Regulation*, OECD   [2]
    Publishing, Paris, http://www.oecd.org/daf/fin (accessed on 19 March 2021).

OECD (Forthcoming), *Compendium of International Organisations' Practices: Working Towards*   [5]
    More Effective International Instruments,
    https://community.oecd.org/servlet/JiveServlet/previewBody/182627-102-1-
    322737/GOV%20RPC%202020%2012.pdf.

1 Why does international regulatory co-operation matter and what is it?

International regulatory co-operation is a key pillar of regulatory policy in an interconnected world. And yet, its full scope and potentials remain often unknown to policymakers and regulators. This chapter aims to familiarise the reader with IRC. It explains why the OECD Regulatory Policy Committee considers it essential to improve the quality of rulemaking and describes the range of mechanisms available to leverage IRC.

Why does international regulatory co-operation matter?

Adapting laws and regulation to an interconnected world

In the past decades, the interconnectedness of countries and the integration of the world economy have increased drastically (Box 1.1), partly due to the many technological revolutions of the past 30 years. The rapid flow of goods, services, people and finance across borders is not least testing the effectiveness and the capacity of domestic regulatory frameworks. If not new, the scale of globalisation combined with the dematerialisation brought by digitalisation increasingly present contemporary policy makers and regulators with challenges that cannot be dealt with in isolation.

The escalation of the COVID-19 crisis into a global pandemic shows how interconnectedness may also have made the world more vulnerable to common threats. It reinforces the need for collective action across policy fronts to supplement domestic action and both tackle the spread of the deadly virus and ensure the flow of essential goods and services (OECD, 2020[1]).

Box 1.1. The evidence of an increasingly interconnected world

We buy goods and services that come from all over the world

Global trade intensity doubled between 1990 and 2015 (measured as the share of the total volume of exports and imports of goods and services in world GDP (OECD, 2017[2]). Today, products cross many borders before they are finally purchased by consumers in a given country (OECD, 2013[3]). Data available for the European Union (EU) shows that cross-border purchases have increased from only 6% of sellers from other EU member states (4% for the rest of the world) in 2008 to 21% (16% for the rest of the world) in 2018 (OECD, 2019[4]).

Yet consumer complaint data shows that growing cross-border transactions online are coupled with an increase in cross-border fraud and sale of unsafe products. In 2018, more than 29 000 international complaints were reported to econsumer.gov, a website dedicated to collecting cross-border complaints (OECD, 2019[4]).

We no longer live in the same place our whole life and travel easily around the world

The total foreign-born population living in OECD countries rose to 129 million people in 2018. On average over all OECD countries, the foreign-born population accounted for 13% of the population in 2018, up from 9.5% in 2000 (OECD, 2019[5]). One in four among 15-year-old students was foreign-born or had at least one foreign-born parent (OECD, 2018[6]).

International passenger travel is increasing globally, and growth is projected to be strongest in developing countries. Global demand for air travel will continue to increase through 2050, with compound annual growth rates of 3.8%. The main drivers are economic growth in developing economies and improving air connectivity. The projected growth rate for global air passenger-kilometer is 4.5% through 2030 and 3.3% through 2050 (ITF, 2019[7])

At the same time that growing travel and trade allow populations worldwide to gain new opportunities and improve their quality of life, increased interdependencies may also have made the world more vulnerable to common threats, as illustrated by the rapid escalation of the COVID-19 pandemic in a global economic and social crisis (OECD, 2020[1]). In 3 months, the virus spread rapidly and led to the brutal stop of economic activity and the lockdown of billions of citizens worldwide.

We use information that comes from many different places

In 2016, about 83% of the adult population in OECD countries had Internet access and 95% of firms registered in OECD countries had high-speed Internet connection (OECD, 2017[2]). Information on Google searches and YouTube viewing revealed an almost universal trend of users increasingly accessing content outside their own country. Data on Paypal's payments show that the Internet is enabling significant cross-border financial transfers on a daily basis (OECD, 2016[8]). The European Commission Impact Assessment accompanying the EU regulation on European Production and Preservation Orders for electronic evidence in criminal matters highlighted that more than half of all investigations involve a cross-border request to access [electronic] evidence (SWD/2018/118 final).

At the same time, information crossing borders thanks to online platforms comes with new risks. Individuals, groups and governments have used online platforms to spread misinformation worldwide, to propagate falsehoods and propaganda for diverse aims, including dividing societies, influencing elections, securing economic gains and recruiting intelligence sources. The growing capabilities of AI and big data analytics allow to propagate, tailor and aim misinformation so that it influences opinions and outcomes faster and more effectively, calling concerted approaches from governments (OECD, 2019[9]).

The rationale for IRC

In such context, IRC may be seen as a necessary strategy to bridge the gap between the domestic nature of rulemaking and the increasingly international dimension of issues that laws and regulations aim to address. As highlighted in (OECD, 1994[10]) and (OECD, 2013[11]), the internationalisation of regulation through co-operation is not new. Practical arrangements for co-operation on laws and regulation have multiplied across jurisdictions and a range of fora – sectoral or regional – established to support dialogues on rules. However, at the exception of a few emblematic systemic examples such the European Union or the Trans-Tasman Mutual Recognition Arrangement, co-operation has mostly followed a path of least resistance with little systematism and overarching strategic vision. In this context, (OECD, 2013[11]) notes that what may be missing is an analytical framework to underpin a clearer understanding of benefits, costs and success factors of the diverse IRC options.

In the face of a lack of data on the benefits and costs of IRC and changing language, the OECD endeavoured to collect evidence and develop the analytical work to support rulemaking. This work has allowed to typify IRC, in particular by broadly defining three main outcomes that IRC may be expected to deliver:

1. **Regulatory effectiveness** – In a context where domestic regulatory frameworks are limited in their reach, IRC may allow addressing challenges beyond a single regulator's jurisdiction, at the (supra-national) level where they may occur.

2. **Economic efficiency** – IRC may limit the undue frictions on international flows that policy makers and regulators may generate when developing and enforcing laws and regulations without considering the international environment.

3. **Administrative efficiency** – IRC may help countries pull intelligence and resources together for issues that may be addressed domestically but may benefit from international intelligence.

The COVID-19 crisis has reinforced this rationale and made particularly apparent the areas in which IRC is needed to achieve successful regulatory outcomes. In line with the general rationale for IRC, the crisis has demonstrated the crucial role of IRC to facilitate the interoperability of services and cross-border activities; to support the resilience of supply chains and enable the availability of essential goods, such as medical and food supplies; and to promote work sharing, mutual learning and pooling of resources between governments to adapt their regulatory policy to face the crisis. These specific needs in the COVID-19 context have highlighted IRC as an important building block of structural regulatory reform, essential to embed resilience in regulatory frameworks and face on-going and future disruptions (including natural disasters, external shocks, disruptive technology, etc.) (OECD, 2020[1]).

It is worth noting that the rationale for IRC may be relevant at various jurisdictional levels. In particular, the relevance of IRC and expected outcomes may equally apply to regulatory co-operation across subnational levels of government in federal states or other national and supra-national jurisdictions where significant regulatory powers may lie at lower levels of governance.

Regulatory effectiveness

IRC allows countries to tackle regulatory challenges at the level where they occur. Climate change, tax evasion and avoidance, financial market instability, pandemics, transboundary pollution or migration flows are all complex and multidimensional issues of intrinsic transnational nature. These are only a few examples of policy challenges where unilateral or unco-ordinated action may lead to outright failures as the ability of countries to effectively deal with them solely through domestic regulation is limited. A failure to address such challenges may be extremely costly for governments, societies and citizens. Conversely, there are striking examples of how joint approaches and rules between countries can lead to tangible impacts in key sectors (Box 1.2).

Box 1.2. International regulatory co-operation in action

- **Eradicating smallpox through collective action led by the WHO.** Smallpox was a deadly disease that killed millions. In the 19th century a vaccine was developed by various countries. It, however, proved ineffective as travellers regularly spread disease. In the late 1950s, a co-ordinated global programme to fight the disease was agreed to within the WHO (OECD/WHO, 2016[12]). In 1980, finally, the WHO announced that smallpox had been eradicated.

- **Preserving the ozone layer thanks to a protocol between 46 countries.** The Montreal Protocol on Substances that Deplete the Ozone Layer (1987), one of the most successful multilateral treaties in the history of the United Nations, led to the reduction of over 97% of all global consumption of controlled ozone depleting substances.

- **Limiting tax evasion thanks to close co-operation between tax authorities.** The OECD Global Forum on Transparency and Exchange of Information for Tax Purposes has changed the paradigm for transparency in tax matters, by introducing automatic exchange of information between tax administrations. This is facilitated through the OECD Model Tax Convention (OECD, 2013[13]), which enables the co-ordination of internationally-agreed taxation standards and has formed the basis for some 3 500 bilateral tax treaties.

- **Avoiding regulatory war through co-ordinated capital account policies**: capital controls put in place by individual countries have pervasive effects on capital flow dynamics in other economies (Pasricha et al., 2018[14]), (Giordani, Ruta and Zhu, 2017[15]), (Gori, Lepers and Mehigan, 2020[16]). These spillovers in turn increase the likelihood of new capital controls in the affected economy (Pasricha et al., 2018[14]), (Gori, Lepers and Mehigan, 2020[16]). Since countries increasingly resort to unilateral capital controls in a context of volatile flows (Blanchard, 2017[17]), policy reactions to a first mover may thus degenerate into "regulatory wars" (Jeanne, 2014[18]), (Pereira Da Silva and Chui, 2017[19]), ultimately delivering suboptimal equilibria for global welfare. In this context, stronger international co-ordination of capital account policies can mitigate such negative externalities, through agreements that specify the appropriate use of capital flow instruments. The OECD Code of Liberalisation of

---

Capital Movements (OECD, 2020[20]), introduced in 1961 and most recently revised in 2019, is such an example, providing an established and tested process for transparent international dialogue and co-operation on capital flow management policies.

- **Joint co-operation efforts to curb transboundary air pollution**. The 1991 Canada – United States Air Quality is a flexible framework that includes emission reduction goals for specific air pollutants and sets commitments to align regulations in key areas. The instrument has helped reduce acid rain and ground-level ozone and advance joint scientific and technical co-operation on transboundary air pollution in both countries (Kauffmann and Saffirio, 2020[21]).

- **Early detection of animal diseases to protect animal health and welfare and spread to humans.** As illustrated in the Study in Support of a Future OIE Observatory of Standard Implementation (OECD, 2020[22]), the World Organisation for Animal Health seeks to detect and disclose the status of animal diseases in the world, including diseases shared between animals and humans (zoonoses). This is all the more important that 60% of the pathogens that affect humans are of animal origin. Through a web-based notification tool, the World Animal Health Information System (WAHIS), 182 OIE Member Countries make information on animal diseases in their country public in real-time, as well as the measures taken to control such diseases. The expected outcome of such a shared mechanism is the early detection and prevention of animal diseases that may spread rapidly within and across countries and degenerate into international, and potentially global crisis.

- **Improving water quality, fauna, flora and preventing floods around the Rhine river**: The co-operation promotes, *inter alia*, sustainable development of the Rhine ecosystem, the production of drinking water from the Rhine, and flood prevention. Originally set up between Switzerland, the Netherlands, France, Germany and Luxemburg, the Berne Convention of 1963 gave it a legal basis. The co-operation was subsequently revised and extended to Austria, Liechtenstein, Italy and the Belgian region of Wallonia. The co-operation takes place within the International Commission for the Protection of the Rhine. It takes the form of joint data collection/research, common measures, co-ordination of warning and alert systems and joint monitoring and evaluation of measures. Thanks to this tight co-operation among countries sharing the river, water quality has significantly improved, with 96% of the population connected to a wastewater treatment plant. The number of animal and plant species living in the river have increased and flood prevention measures were implemented (OECD, 2013[23]).

Economic efficiency

Regulating without consideration for the international context is likely to result in unnecessary regulatory fragmentation across countries. While the underlying laws and regulations may not deal with transboundary issues, their divergences across jurisdictions may be costly to businesses, citizens and governments. There are areas where regulatory differences are justified by differing consumer preferences or specific country conditions (geographic or other). There are nevertheless cases where divergences in regulation are purely the results of non-transparent regulatory practices and regulators working in isolation. In these instances, some of the unnecessary costs of regulatory divergences may be addressed to limit frictions on international flows – trade, investment, capital or other.

OECD research shows that for example, costs to traders may be organised in 3 categories (OECD, 2017[24]): 1) the costs to identify the relevant regulatory requirements; 2) the costs to adapt their production processes to comply with them; and 3) the costs to prove conformity to a variety of administrations in various jurisdictions (Figure 1.1).

In the financial sector, regulatory divergences are "perceived" to cost financial institutions between 5 to 10% of their annual global turnover (some USD 780 billion per year), with the financial performance of smaller firms the hardest hit (IFAC/BIAC, 2018[25]).

Figure 1.1. Heterogeneity-related trade costs for producers and traders

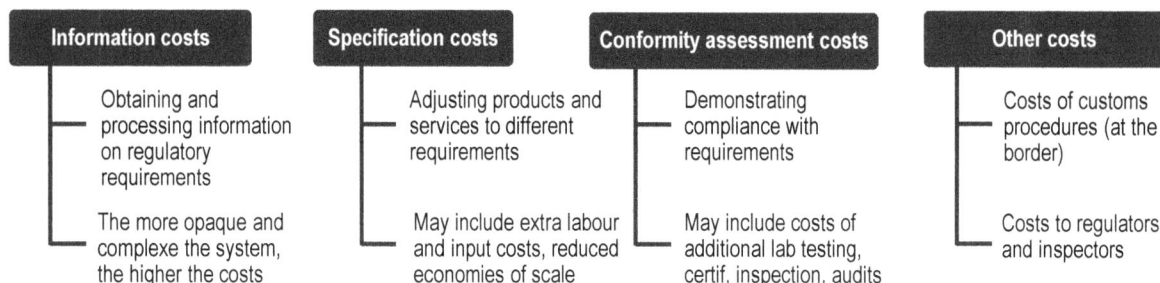

Information costs	Specification costs	Conformity assessment costs	Other costs
Obtaining and processing information on regulatory requirements	Adjusting products and services to different requirements	Demonstrating compliance with requirements	Costs of customs procedures (at the border)
The more opaque and complexe the system, the higher the costs	May include extra labour and input costs, reduced economies of scale	May include costs of additional lab testing, certif, inspection, audits	Costs to regulators and inspectors

Source: (OECD, 2017[24]), "International Regulatory Co-operation and Trade: Understanding the Trade Costs of Regulatory Divergence and the Remedies", OECD Publishing, Paris, https://dx.doi.org/10.1787/9789264275942-en.

Administrative efficiency

IRC improves the capacities of domestic regulators through peer learning, sharing of resources and capacity to benefit from existing evidence/expertise instead through the gathering of international intelligence (Box 1.3). Regulation requires significant expertise and resources to gather the relevant evidence and a functioning regulatory infrastructure for rule development and implementation. It is increasingly difficult for countries and their regulators to afford this expertise. Yet, the complexity of contemporary challenges makes effective and efficient regulatory regimes based on science and solid evidence more crucial than ever. When regulators from different jurisdictions co-operate, they can share their experience, expertise and resources, increase the pool of evidence and practices they can draw from, confront their policy choices and learn lessons from jurisdictions with a track record, thus reducing the overall costs of good regulation. In addition, co-ordination in implementation can further help ensure consistency in application and prevent regulatory arbitrage (OECD, 2010[26]).

Box 1.3. Examples of administrative efficiency gains from IRC

OECD Mutual Acceptance of Data (MAD)

For example, the OECD Mutual Acceptance of Data (MAD) [OECD/LEGAL/0194 and OECD/LEGAL/0252] helps save more than EUR 309 million per year through reduced chemical testing and the harmonisation of chemical safety tools and policies across jurisdictions (OECD, 2019[27]). The co-operation has brought health and environmental gains from Adherents being able to evaluate and manage more chemicals than they would if worked independently, and represents a rare case in which the benefits and costs of international regulatory co-operation have been assessed quantitatively, demonstrating how this co-operation can support administrative efficiency.

Multilateral Convention to Implement Tax Treaty Related Measures to Prevent BEPS (MLI)

The Multilateral Convention to Implement Tax Treaty Related Measures to Prevent BEPS (MLI) that entered into force in July 2018 allowed parties to transpose results from the OECD/G20 Base Erosion and Profit Shifting Project (BEPS) into more than 1 650 tax treaties worldwide. The MLI save governments from multiple bilateral negotiations and renegotiations to implement the tax treaty

---

changes needed as a result of the measures agreed under BEPS. The MLI currently has 95 signatories or parties from all continents and all levels of development.

European Medicines Agency (EMA)

The European medicines regulatory system is based on a network of around 50 regulatory authorities from the 31 European Economic Area countries, the European Commission and the European Medicines Agency (EMA). EMA works with national bodies in the regulation and licensing of medicines and medical devices and monitoring of their safety. Based on the single EU regulatory system for pharmaceuticals, confidential information is exchanged between the EU member states and results of inspections carried out by any of the EU member states are automatically recognised by all. According to EMA, this regulatory system offers inter alia the following benefits:

- Enables member states to pool resources, expertise and co-ordinate work to regulate medicines. In 2019, for example, EMA recommended the authorisation of 66 new medicines for human use;
- Reduces the administrative burden through the centralised authorisation procedure, helping medicines to reach patients faster;
- Accelerates the exchange of information on important issues, such as the safety of medicines.

Source: (OECD, 2013[13]) and *"Information Brochure: Multilateral Convention to Implement Tax Treaty Related Measures to Prevent BEPS"*, OECD, 2020, available at www.oecd.org/tax/treaties/multilateral-instrument-BEPS-tax-treaty-information-brochure.pdf, (OECD, 2013[11]), (OECD, 2016[28]), www.ema.europa.eu/en/about-us/how-we-work/european-medicines-regulatory-network and www.ema.europa.eu/en/documents/annual-report/2019-annual-report-european-medicines-agency_en.pdf.

Identifying the opportunities for IRC

While it can be argued that a minimum level of "international awareness" is essential to ensure the quality of domestic rulemaking, stronger forms of IRC require more than awareness and do not come free. The efforts and investment they impose to develop and maintain and their costs and potential negative side effects need to be assessed against the expected benefits (as essential that they may be) to make an informed co-operation decision. It is all the more important to identify a range of forms that IRC can take (see section 3), with various benefits and costs.

Broadly speaking, and in line with the rationale for IRC delineated above, OECD research shows that the benefits of IRC can be understood as encompassing four dimensions: 1) the economic gains from reduced costs on economic activity and increased trade, investment and financial flows; 2) the progress in managing risks and externalities across borders; 3) the administrative efficiency from greater transparency and work-sharing across governments and public authorities; as well as 4) the knowledge flow and peer learning accruing from co-operation.

In turn, the potential costs of and obstacles to IRC relate to: 1) the burdens of and resources entailed with developing and maintaining the co-operation; 2) the distance from a jurisdiction's own regulatory "optimum" and the rigidities that the co-operation may generate; 3) the loss of sovereignty (real or perceived) accompanying the consensus building and other challenges raised by the political economy of co-operation; and 4) implementation bottlenecks.

Both the expected benefits and costs/challenges of IRC are explained in further details in (OECD, 2013[11]). They are also declined according to the type of IRC considered – indeed, both the gains in terms of regulatory effectiveness, economic and administrative efficiency and the burdens, challenges and resistance that may be encountered highly depend on the types of IRC approaches considered. Annex A summarises the findings from (OECD, 2013[11]). In the end, whether the benefits outweigh the costs in specific instances will hinge on various elements, including the sector of interest, the characteristics of the countries involved in the partnership, and the co-operation approach under consideration. To further compound the complexity of assessing the benefits and costs, some of the benefits may not be easily appropriable by countries and while IRC may be beneficial overall, the allocation of gains may vary across jurisdictions.

Regardless of the complexity, OECD research suggests that IRC is a necessary feature of successful policies in areas that share certain features (OECD, 1994[10]), in particular:

1. Areas that are essentially science driven, based on irrefutable facts (e.g. chemical testing) and that benefit from shared methodologies;

2. Areas involving global "goods" or "bads" where problems have an intrinsic cross-border nature and cannot be solved by individual governments, such as global warming, air pollution, banking and finance, pandemics, among other; and

3. Areas for which there is a strong incentive to co-operate, e.g. an unambiguous commercial or economic motivation (typically trade, international investment or financial markets) or where countries can benefit from sharing information (health and safety domains); and where the disincentives to co-operate are limited or can be managed (e.g. the possibility of free riding, i.e. that some countries derive the benefits without incurring the cost of co-operating for example).

There are a number of key drivers of IRC, such as geographical proximity, economic interdependence, and the maturity of regulatory policy in the partners that shape these IRC efforts either enhancing or creating obstacles to their effective delivery (Box 1.4). In addition, the success of IRC is also subject to domestic political economy considerations including the existence of high-level commitment across the political cycle to collaborate with other countries, willingness to deploy resources in advancing regulatory co-operation and building technical capacities these effects, among other.

Box 1.4. Drivers of IRC

A number of factors promote, hinder and shape IRC endeavours. These hypotheses may inform policy makers pondering about when, how and with whom to engage in IRC. They do not represent, however, static rules on the political economy of IRC and may be more or less relevant depending on the sector or policy issue addressed.

- Geographical proximity: geographical proximity may increase the need and likelihood of co-operation and IRC due to joint challenges, and potentially (but not systematically) similar worldviews and preferences.

- Economic interdependence: high trade volumes and other economic interdependencies are likely to increase the likelihood for co-operation so as to lock in a certain level of regulatory openness and to lower trade costs through the dismantling of unnecessary regulatory divergence.

- Economic properties of partners: the respective economic size of partners may impact their respective capacity to impose their own approach. From this perspective, the evidence shows that IRC is easier between economies of different sizes, where there are obvious "rule-makers" and "rule-takers" rather than between economies of similar sizes and regulatory expectations. In these cases, the availability of international instruments may facilitate IRC by offering a common anchor outside of the two partners.

- Nature of the regulated area: the political sensitivity of measures subject to regulation – i.e. their inherent risk levels or social and economic nature – may significantly affect the likelihood of IRC. IRC on politically sensitive measures should be more difficult than IRC on less sensitive measures. Depending on the sector, there may also be more or less inter-state competition and free riding dynamics hindering IRC.

- Proximity and maturity of domestic regulatory governance: factors such as the proximity of rulemaking systems and practices and shared legal and cultural heritage are likely to increase the trust of partners in their respective frameworks and therefore provide incentives to regulators to co-operate. The success of IRC also hinges on the maturity of the respective regulatory policy and governance of partners, including the transparency of regulatory governance, the ability of states to enforce regulation and the commitment to IRC at the domestic level. Those are all factors likely to improve the confidence of regulators in the capacity of their peers in foreign jurisdictions to uphold their regulatory standards across borders.

Source: Elaborated from Basedow and Kauffmann (2016), "The Political Economy of International Regulatory Co-operation: A theoretical framework to understand international regulatory co-operation", OECD, Paris, unpublished Working Paper (Kauffmann and Basedow, 2016[29]).

Figure 1.2. IRC decision checklist

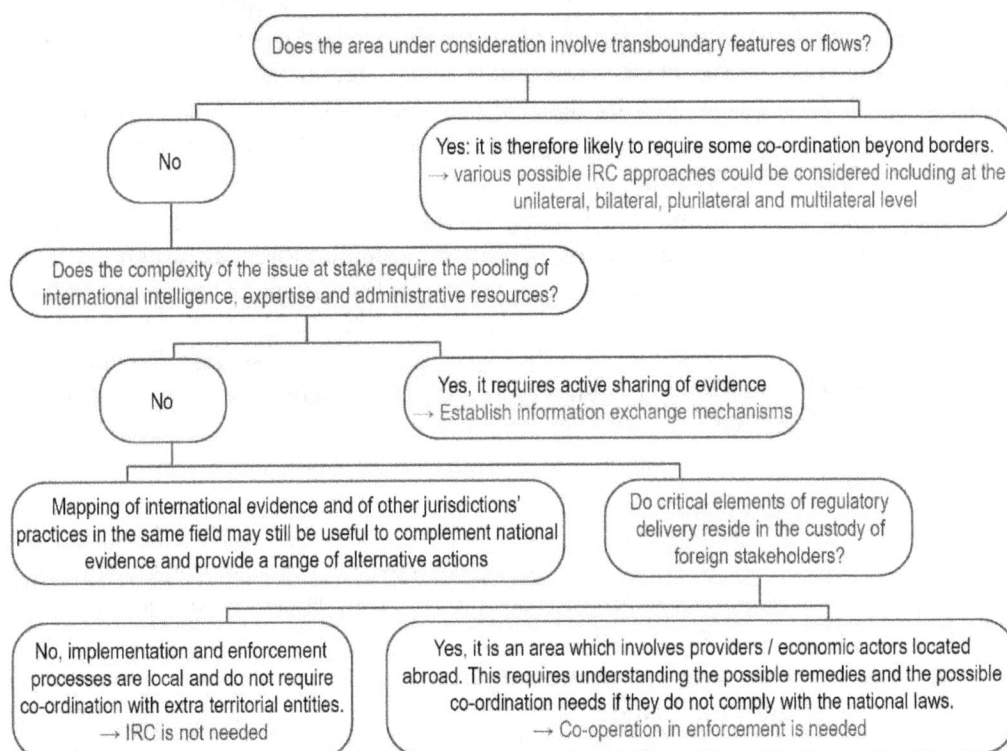

Source: Author's own elaboration.

Building on these various characteristics, it is possible to help policy makers navigate the intricacies of IRC and decide on the relevance of IRC in their own field with the support of a synthetic checklist of the key considerations to take into account. While this checklist may need further development and could become a standalone decision tool, a simple decision tree could be structured around the following key questions:

- Does the area under consideration involve trans-boundary features or flows?
- Does the complexity of the issue at stake require the pooling of international intelligence, expertise and administrative resources?

- Do critical elements of regulatory delivery reside in the custody of foreign stakeholders?

The decision to engage in IRC and the type of IRC to be considered would then depend on the answers provided to these questions, a process that is synthesised in the following flow chart above (Figure 1.2).

What is international regulatory co-operation?

Definition and terminology

International Regulatory Co-operation (IRC) is about promoting the interoperability of legal and regulatory frameworks. Based on (OECD, 2013[11]), it can be defined as covering "Any agreement or organisational arrangement, formal or informal, between countries to promote some form of co-operation in the design, monitoring, enforcement, or *ex post* management of regulation". This is in line with the definition adopted in a number of countries (Box 1.5).

There are several implications to this broad definition:

- **First**, **IRC is not restricted to its strict equivalence with international legal obligations, but also includes non-binding agreements and voluntary approaches**. This is exemplified by the wide range of activities in support of consensus building and joint rulemaking provided by international organisations, as well as the variety of international instruments they develop, most of which non-legally binding, and that form the international ecosystem of rules (OECD, 2019[30]). It is also illustrated by the multiplicity of non-binding and voluntary bilateral or plurilateral initiatives that exist across regulators from different jurisdictions supported by Memoranda of Understanding.[1]

- **Second, IRC is not limited to the design phase of the regulatory governance cycle, but importantly includes the downstream side of implementation, enforcement, and *ex post* management of regulation**. There are a number of illustrations of this, including the Canada-US Regulatory Cooperation Council (RCC) (OECD, 2013[31]), which shows that even when policy objectives and rules may be quite align, frictions may arise from diverging enforcement procedures that need to be tackled through on-going discussions. The case of Competition Law Enforcement (OECD, 2013[13]) also demonstrates the importance of exchange of information and co-operation in the remediation of competition cases, an area where international co-operation on enforcement has been increasing since 2012, under the impetus of international fora such as OECD and the International Competition Network (OECD/ICN, 2021[32]). Similarly, co-operation on enforcement proves essential also in the area of consumer safety, typically facilitate enforcement of product safety issues across jurisdictions (OECD, 2013[13]) (OECD, Forthcoming[33]).

- **The focus on "co-operation" in the definition should not hide or minimise the critical importance of unilateral action** to promote interoperability of regulatory frameworks and regulatory coherence internationally and establish solid foundations for collaboration across jurisdictions on regulatory matters. Hence the consideration of unilateral approaches in the OECD typology of IRC instruments, which closely follows the parallel efforts of a number of countries.[2] Unilateral actions may involve directly adopting the regulations or recognising regulatory outcomes or decisions of another jurisdiction or international standards, or applying the regulatory disciplines that will put pressure towards greater regulatory coherence. As such they directly contribute to the objectives of IRC, i.e. to facilitate regulatory interoperability to achieve policy objectives.

Box 1.5. Selected country definitions of international regulatory co-operation

A number of countries provide a definition of international regulatory co-operation and make them available on their websites.

Canada (Treasury Board): Regulatory co-operation is a process where governments work together to:

- reduce unnecessary regulatory differences;
- eliminate duplicative requirements and processes;
- harmonise or align regulations;
- share information and experiences; and
- adopt international standards.

Regulatory co-operation applies to a range of regulatory activities, including: policy development; inspections; certification; adoption and development of standards; and product and testing approvals.

New Zealand (Ministry of Business, Innovation and Employment): International regulatory cooperation is the different ways that regulators from different countries work together to discuss, develop, manage or enforce regulations.

United States (Executive Order 13609 of 1 May 2012): "International regulatory cooperation" refers to a bilateral, regional, or multilateral process [...] in which national governments engage in various forms of collaboration and communication with respect to regulations, in particular a process that is reasonably anticipated to lead to the development of significant regulations.

In addition to these generic definitions of IRC, a number of trade agreements with dedicated chapters on regulatory policy and co-operation provide working definitions of IRC adopted solely for the purpose of the agreement. These definitions are not directly comparable as they reflect the different scope and focus of each chapter.

Agreement between New Zealand–Singapore on a Closer Economic Partnership (CEP Upgrade): "Regulatory cooperation activities means the efforts between the Parties to enhance regulatory cooperation in order to further domestic policy objectives, improve the effectiveness of domestic regulation in the face of increased cross-border activity and promote international trade and investment, economic growth and employment."

United States-Mexico-Canada Agreement (USMCA): "Regulatory cooperation means an effort between two or more Parties to prevent, reduce, or eliminate unnecessary regulatory differences to facilitate trade and promote economic growth, while maintaining or enhancing standards of public health and safety and environmental protection."

Source:www.whitehouse.gov/sites/whitehouse.gov/files/omb/inforeg/inforeg/eo_13609/eo13609_05012012.pdf; www.canada.ca/en/treasury-board-secretariat/services/regulatory-cooperation/learn-about-regulatory-cooperation.html; www.mbie.govt.nz/cross-government-functions/regulatory-stewardship/international-regulatory-cooperation; and (Kauffmann and Saffirio, 2021[34]).

IRC has become a critical dimension of regulatory quality and effectiveness, as illustrated by the inclusion of a principle on IRC in the 2012 Recommendation (OECD, 2012[35]). In the past two to three decades, in a context of continuous reduction in tariffs and rise of global value chains, trade policy makers have also paid increased attention to the costs accruing to traders from non-tariff measures (NTMs) and regulatory divergences across jurisdictions. As such, different tools of regulatory policy, including IRC, are embedded in the WTO context, in particular in the WTO frameworks on Technical Barriers to Trade (TBT) and the Application of Sanitary and Phytosanitary (SPS) (OECD/WTO, 2019[36]) (OECD, 2017[24]) and increasingly as horizontal chapters in bilateral and regional trade agreements (Kauffmann and Saffirio, 2021[34]).

However, terminology varies to a certain extent depending on the actors discussing it and the objectives it pursues (Box 1.6).

IRC encompasses a multiplicity of approaches, which are united by their focus on enhancing the interoperability of laws, regulations and regulatory frameworks. This includes a range of 'softer' activities beyond the development of rules, such as exchanging information and participating in international fora, which form the building blocks of rulemaking and regulatory co-operation. However, it is important to separate IRC from the other multiple forms of co-operation that may exist. In particular, precluded from the IRC definition are forms of co-operation that do not relate to or support the rule-making process, such as those involving the provision of development aid, project funding or capacity building.

Box 1.6. Regulatory policy, good regulatory practices and international regulatory co-operation: bridging the language gaps between regulatory and trade policymakers

Despite common interests in improving the effectiveness and efficiency of regulation, the regulatory community and the trade policy community tend to use different language and tools, relative to their respective mandates and scope of activities. This applies to the broad agenda itself, as exemplified in the examples of language in Table 1.1, as well as for the individual tools of regulatory policy.

Table 1.1. Terminology used in relation to regulatory policy

OECD	WTO TBT Committee	Other terminologies used in countries
Regulatory quality Regulatory reform Regulatory policy	Good regulatory practice	Better Regulation Smart regulation Regulatory fitness deregulation Paperwork reduction Regulatory management Regulatory governance Regulatory improvement Regulatory Coherence Simplification

Source: adapted from (OECD, 2015[37]).

In the context of the WTO, the SPS and the TBT Agreements in particular aim to ensure that technical regulations, conformity assessment procedures, standards and SPS measures are transparent, non-discriminatory and do not result in unnecessary barriers to trade. While GRPs and regulatory quality are not explicitly mentioned in these Agreements, GRPs are commonly referred to in the work of TBT and SPS Committees. The TBT Committee has recognised the importance of GRP for reducing technical barriers to trade, through "improved and effective implementation of the substantive obligations of the TBT Agreement."[1]

In the context of the TBT Agreement, regulatory co-operation is aimed at limiting costs arising from divergences in product regulations between countries, while respecting differences in regulatory objectives. In the TBT Committee, members have highlighted that regulatory co-operation can help achieve a better understanding of different regulatory systems and approaches to addressing identified needs, and can promote regulatory convergence, harmonisation, mutual recognition and equivalence, thereby contributing to the avoidance of unnecessary regulatory differences. IRC is recognised as an element of good regulatory practice.

[1] G/TBT/26, 13 November 2009, para. 5.
Source: (OECD/WTO, 2019[36]).

Given the variability in language and the importance to clearly separate IRC from the multiple other forms of international co-operation that may exist clearly point to the need for clear definitions and delineation of concepts. These OECD Best Practice Principles aim to help with such objective. Box 1.7 synthesises the key IRC concepts in short definitions.

Box 1.7. Glossary of key terms related to IRC

Due to the multiplicity of actors involved in IRC, the exact terminology used varies and is not subject to internationally agreed definitions. For the purpose of the RPC work on IRC, the following terms are used without prejudice of the meaning they can have in individual countries and international organisations, including the OECD:

- **International regulatory co-operation (IRC)** can broadly be referred to as *"any agreement, formal or informal, between countries to promote some form of co-operation in the design, monitoring, enforcement or ex-post management of regulation."* (OECD, 2013[11]).

- **International organisation.** The academic literature acknowledges their diversity and offers several classifications based on functions, membership or objective (OECD, 2016[28]). For the purpose of the Partnership of International Organisations for Effective International Rulemaking, the term has been defined by the OECD broadly to encompass a variety of organisations engaged in normative activities, i.e. the development and management of "rules" regardless of their mandate, sector, legal attributes or nature. These organisations share 3 critical features: 1) they generate rules, be they legal, policy or technical instruments/standards; 2) they rely on a secretariat; and 3) they are international in that they involve "representatives" from several countries.

- **International Standards.** The term used in this document follows the World Trade Organization TBT Committee Decision on international standards[1] which set out six principles for the development of international standards, including: i) transparency; ii) openness; iii) impartiality and consensus; iv) effectiveness and relevance; v) coherence; and vi) the development dimension. In addition, WTO case-law provides some guidance. According to such case law, for an instrument to be considered an "international standard" under the TBT Agreement it must both: constitute a "standard" (i.e. a document approved by a recognised body, that provides, for common and repeated use, rules, guidelines or characteristics for products or related processes and production methods, with which compliance is not mandatory) and be "international" in character, i.e. adopted by an international standardising body.[2]

- **International instruments.** The normative work of international organisations goes beyond international standards. Therefore, to encompass the broader range of legal and policy documents adopted by international organisations, and in line with the approach used in (OECD, 2019[38]) this document refers to the broader term of **international instruments** as covering legally binding requirements that are meant to be directly binding on the international organisations' members and non-legally binding instruments that may be given binding value through transposition in domestic legislation or recognition in international legal instruments. This broad notion therefore covers e.g. treaties, legally binding decisions, non-legally binding recommendations, model treaties or laws, declarations and voluntary international standards.[1]

- **International rulemaking (in the context of international organisations).** For the purpose of this document, and consistently with the analytical work led by the OECD on the topic since 2014 (OECD, 2019[38]),"international rulemaking" encompasses the design,

---

development, implementation and enforcement of international instruments (see above) by governments or other actors via the international organisations of which they are members, or by the Secretariats of the international organisations based on mandates received from their members, regardless of their legal status, effects or attributes and of the nature of the organisation (public or private). This definition does not prejudge the domestic use of this term by countries.

[1] This broader approach is chosen as it can be applicable regardless of the thematic/sectoral scope of the international standards. This differs from the approach of the SPS Agreement, which defines international standards, guidelines and recommendations based on whether they come from any of the following three international bodies: international standards for "food safety" established by the FAO/WHO "Codex Alimentarius Commission" (Codex); international standards for "animal health and zoonoses" developed by the "World Organisation for Animal Health" (OIE); international standards for "plant health" developed under the auspices of the "International Plant Protection Convention" (IPPC). For matters not covered by the above organizations, the SPS Agreement also allows for the possibility of the SPS Committee identifying "appropriate standards, guidelines and recommendations promulgated by other relevant international organizations open for membership to all Members".

[2] See, e.g. Appellate Body Report in US – Tuna II and Panel Report in Australia – Tobacco Plain Packaging (currently under appeal). The TBT Committee decision on the six Principles for the Development of International Standards, Guides and Recommendations (G/TBT/9, 13 November 2000, para. 20 and Annex 4) also played an important role for clarifying the meaning of "international standard" under the TBT Agreement (see e.g. Appellate Body Report in US – Tuna II , paras. 370-379 and 382, 384, and 394). The TBT Agreement refers to "relevant" international standards; the term relevant has been addressed by the Appellate Body in EC-Sardines. For further discussion on the "Six Principles", see pp. 80-81.

Source: (OECD, 2017[24]) (OECD, 2019[30]) (OECD/WTO, 2019[36]).

The variety of international regulatory co-operation approaches

OECD work shows the multiplicity of approaches to facilitate the interoperability of regulatory frameworks. They may cover activities from the exchange of information to the harmonisation of rules. They may focus on the stage preceding the development of rules – such as the evidence gathering – or apply to the regulatory delivery side (in enforcement/inspection for example). They may involve specific institutional arrangements or rely on peer to peer agreements. De facto, they take the form of a continuum of complementary mechanisms ranging from unilateral to international multilateral action (Figure 1.3), rather than a discrete set of mutually exclusive options (as illustrated by the New Zealand IRC Toolkit).

The complementarity of IRC mechanisms is well illustrated by the coexistence and layering of mechanisms at sector/policy issue level. The co-operation to address air pollution provides a good example encompassing the unilateral adoption of international environmental standards; bilateral memorandum of understanding (MoU) on data exchange, technical assistance and capacity building; and engagement in multilateral environmental programmes and fora, plurilateral research projects, and joint ministerial meetings (Kauffmann and Saffirio, 2020[21]). Competition law enforcement provides another illustration of the layering of IRC mechanisms in the same field, involving a mixture of competition and non-specific instruments, both formal and informal co-operation mechanisms between different levels of government (OECD, 2013[11]). Several IRC mechanisms also complement each other in the area of consumer protection enforcement co-operation – which relies on binding international agreements (such as high-level government-to-government agreements), non-binding memoranda of understanding and other agency-to-agency agreements, as well as informal exchanges through peer-to-peer agency networks (such as the International Consumer Protection Enforcement Network) and staff exchanges (OECD, Forthcoming[33]).

Figure 1.3. IRC mechanisms

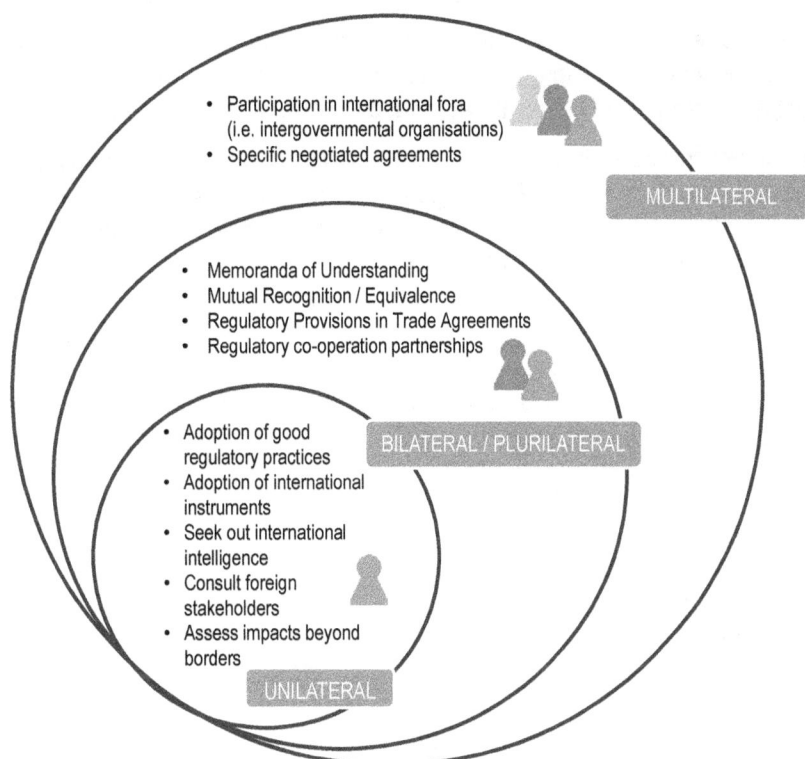

- Participation in international fora
  (i.e. intergovernmental organisations)
- Specific negotiated agreements

MULTILATERAL

- Memoranda of Understanding
- Mutual Recognition / Equivalence
- Regulatory Provisions in Trade Agreements
- Regulatory co-operation partnerships

BILATERAL / PLURILATERAL

- Adoption of good
  regulatory practices
- Adoption of international
  instruments
- Seek out international
  intelligence
- Consult foreign
  stakeholders
- Assess impacts beyond
  borders

UNILATERAL

Source: Adapted from OECD (2013), International Regulatory Co-operation: Addressing Global Challenges, OECD Publishing, Paris, https://dx.doi.org/10.1787/9789264200463-en.

Domestically, the interoperability of regulatory frameworks can be improved unilaterally by investing in the quality of regulation and integrating considerations of the international environment

Countries can do a lot domestically to improve the coherence of their regulatory frameworks with the international environment, build trustworthy institutions that can form the foundation of co-operation arrangements and establish the conditions and support for beneficial co-ordination with foreign jurisdictions. The range of practices and disciplines highlighted in the 2012 Recommendation and the 2005 APEC-OECD Integrated Checklist on Regulatory Reform (APEC-OECD, 2005[39]) provides a strong basis to improve the quality of domestic rulemaking and embed more systematic considerations of the international environment.

On this last point, principle 12 of the 2012 Recommendation promotes these unilateral practices likely to support the interoperability of regulatory frameworks and detailed in the Best Practice Principles, in short:

- Considering systematically the intelligence accumulated in other jurisdictions on similar issues to inform the rationale and range of potential options
- Adopting international instruments and other relevant regulatory frameworks when developing or updating laws and regulations, or detailing the rationale for diverting from them
- Facilitating the engagement of stakeholders beyond the jurisdiction to gather information about the implications of domestic regulation
- Assessing the range of impacts (including on international flows and outside the jurisdiction) of laws and regulations once they are adopted and their divergence with international good practice.

These unilateral good regulatory practices provide an essential first step and building block of IRC – beyond helping to avoid the unnecessary regulatory divergences through better informed rulemaking, they foster the mutual knowledge and confidence needed across jurisdictions for stronger forms of IRC. They, however, do not in themselves necessarily ensure the expected outcome of IRC, which may require going beyond unilateral action and entering bilateral, regional or international forms of co-operation.

Recent OECD work on IRC responses to the COVID-19 crisis shows that some governments have opted to unilaterally uphold technical standards for medical devices issued by competent authorities in other jurisdictions (OECD, 2020[11]). Such unilateral recognition has proved a flexible and rapid option for countries seeking to secure the availability of critical medical products. As an example, the US Food and Drug Administration (US FDA) waived in April 2020 certain regulatory requirements to authorise healthcare personnel to use the disposable respirators (masks) that met requirements approved in other countries, even if not approved by the National Institute for Occupational Safety and Health (NIOSH) (US Food and Drug Administration, 2020[67]). Health Canada has set up simplified importation and sale procedures on medical devices necessary for use in relation to COVID-19, if they have been granted market approval by a foreign regulatory authority (Health Canada, 2020[68]).

There is a multiplicity of potential co-operation modalities and institutional arrangements, at the bilateral, regional and multilateral levels

There is no simple way to illustrate the range of possible co-operation approaches, all the more that they may combine different features and vary across sectors and countries – the range of IRC mechanisms and their complexity is described in details in (OECD, 2013[11]) and the accompanying case studies (listed in Annex B). One way to capture the broad variety of mechanisms in a schematic way is to differentiate between those that involve the harmonisation of rules as the basis for interoperability and those that preserve the variety of regulatory frameworks and seek to build bridges across them. They are represented in a simplified and not exhaustive way in Figure 1.4.

Figure 1.4. Non-exhaustive categorisation of types of IRC by outcome

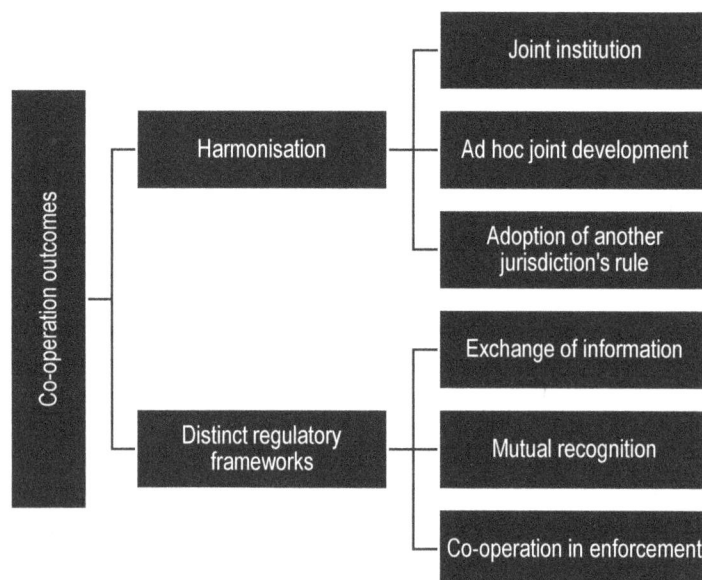

Regulatory harmonisation

Regulatory harmonisation (defined as the adoption of joint rules across two or more jurisdictions) does away with regulatory divergence between participating countries at its very root, i.e. in the design stage. It should thereby significantly increase the effectiveness and efficiency of regulation across partners by limiting the margin for interpretation and the frictions arising from divergences. Examples include the development of Regulations and Directives in the European Union, as exemplified by the evolution of the European Union Energy Regulation (OECD, 2013[31]), as well as the harmonisation case described in the Study of the Equipment Energy Efficiency (E3) Programme between Australia and New Zealand (Kauffmann and Saffirio, 2020[21]).

As illustrated by these examples, "regulatory harmonisation" covers in practice different realities and different depths of co-operation, i.e. the adoption of another jurisdiction's rule, the joint adoption of a common rule through deliberative process in a joint institution, the joint adoption of common rules without the involvement of a joint institution, or the joint reference to a third rule-maker (typically an international organisation). There is also a misperception in regulatory harmonisation that common rules mean seamless enforcement, which is rarely the case. EU Directives for example are developed through joint institutions and mean to apply in all EU members. However, contrary to EU regulations that are directly applicable, their implementation involves their transposition in domestic legislation – leaving some margins for divergence – and empowers the EU member states for their enforcement. OECD work on regulatory enforcement and inspections show that there can be significant differences in enforcement approaches that may create important costs to regulated entities and/or affect the effectiveness of regulation.

The work of the Partnership of International Organisations for Effective International Rulemaking shows that the majority of international instruments (meant to provide for regulatory harmonisation) allow for flexible implementation and adaptation to specific context – they are rarely applicable directly and a significant share is voluntary in nature (see below).

This begs the question of why not apply one single regulation and delivery to all? Harmonisation can come with important costs. It limits the regulatory sovereignty of countries. In its extreme forms, public administrations no longer develop regulation and standards at the domestic level, but transpose international measures. The development of joint approaches may fail to account for the variety of specific conditions and to satisfy the needs and expectations of singular domestic administrations and citizens. Harmonisation involves by definition uniformity and this may not be the best solution in all contexts. This may also stifle innovation in regulatory approaches.

There is therefore a balance to strike between full regulatory harmonisation (that can be caricatured as one rule, one enforcement) that effectively erases the costs of (even small) differences in interpretation and application of rules and the flexibility that a more lax system of adoption of soft international instruments may allow.

Equivalence/mutual recognition: the alternative to regulatory harmonisation?

A number of IRC mechanisms different to regulatory harmonisation promote regulatory alignment while allowing room for regulatory diversity; these include "equivalence" and mutual recognition mechanisms. There is a wide spectrum of mutual recognition modalities identified in (Correia de Brito, Kauffmann and Pelkmans, 2016[40]), ranging from the recognition of regulatory outcomes of different rules to the more limited recognition of conformity assessment results embodied in different agreements (Figure 1.5). Mutual recognition of rules is rarely used except in the European Union, between Australia and New Zealand in the Trans-Tasman Mutual recognition Arrangement and in a number of specific limited cases (such as the EU-US organic equivalence).

Figure 1.5. Spectrum of mutual recognition modalities

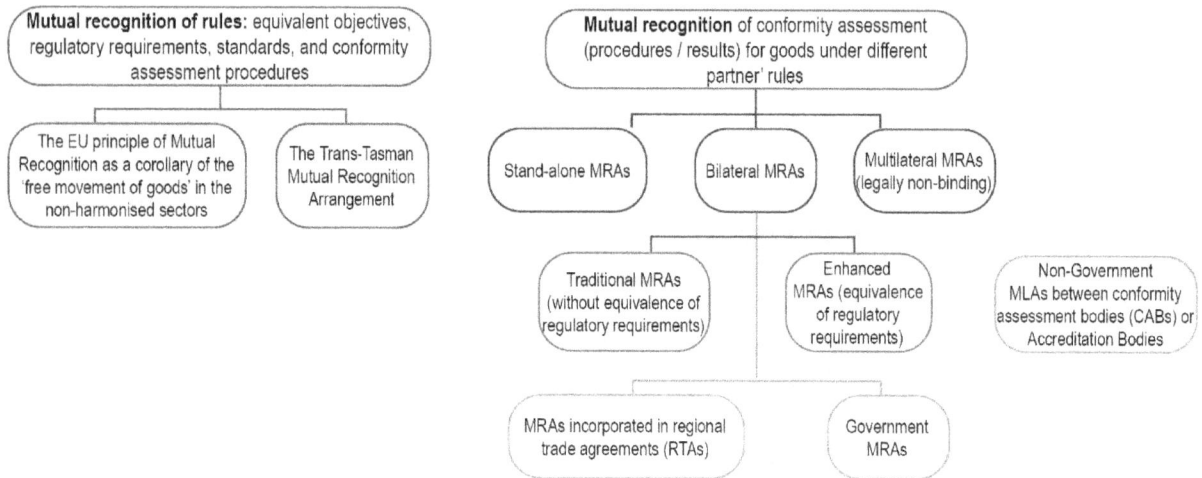

Source: (Correia de Brito, Kauffmann and Pelkmans, 2016[40]).

In most cases, countries adopt recognition of their conformity assessment procedures, i.e. the capability of conformity assessment bodies to test and certify against the rules and procedures of another country. The purpose of these Mutual Recognition Agreements (MRAs) is to facilitate market access by eliminating duplicative testing and certification or inspection, reducing the uncertainty about a possible rejection and shortening 'time-to-market'.

The OECD Mutual Acceptance of Data (MAD) presents another case where the "recognition" focuses on chemical test data. It shows the potential benefits of mutual recognition of results when scaled up to the multilateral level (OECD, 2013[13]). There are also examples of co-operation taking place through mutual assistance in the enforcement stage as established by the study of co-operation among competition authorities (OECD, 2013[13]), and in the area of consumer protection (OECD, Forthcoming[33]).

There is limited systematic and quantified evidence on the performance of mutual recognition. In the area of the recognition of the equivalence of regulatory outcomes, the Trans-Tasman Mutual Recognition Arrangement stands out with its regular assessments carried out by the Australian Productivity Commission.[3] There is also some academic literature on MRAs. It shows that they do away with the need for multiple conformity assessments and shorten the time needed to trade goods across borders. They have some positive impacts on trade especially in science-driven sectors with long global value chains, where sufficient economic gains are expected such as telecoms equipment, machinery and electronic equipment. However, MRAs are also costly to negotiate and to maintain. They require the continuous co-operation between national regulators. (Correia de Brito, Kauffmann and Pelkmans, 2016[40]) shows that MRAs only deliver in sectors with limited regulatory divergence (for example where a strong international standard provides for common regulatory grounds such as in the electronic/electric area) and in country relationships with high levels of trust and confidence in the respective regulatory and administrative systems.

The role for trade agreements?

Countries have been using trade agreements as a vehicle to promote the effectiveness and efficiency of regulation by including provisions related to good regulatory practices and international regulatory co-operation (OECD, 2017[24]). This is not a new trend. Over the past decades, a number of agreements have included language related to GRP and/or IRC mechanisms, in particular reflecting and sometimes deepening WTO disciplines set out in the TBT and SPS Agreements and Committees (OECD/WTO, 2019[36]). These provisions promote traditional good regulatory practices around transparency and evidence based rule-making. Trade agreements also provide a path for mutual recognition and act as vehicles for other mechanisms that promote dialogue and encourage parties to the agreements to initiate co-operation on regulatory matters. In addition, some agreements also include annexes or chapters to include sector-specific commitments around regulatory management tools, use of international standards, implementation of mutual recognition or other forms of regulatory alignment.

More recently, trade agreements have become more detailed and ambitious in the content and scope of GRP and IRC provisions. In particular, a number of trade agreements have incorporated dedicated chapters on GRPs and/or IRC (Kauffmann and Saffirio, 2021[34]). While, it is too early to assess the overall impact of these dedicated chapters for regulatory quality and IRC, a number of considerations can already be highlighted based on their content and initial implementation steps.

The level of ambition of these standalone chapters is largely connected to the state of play of regulatory policy in partner countries. Yet their increasing incorporation in trade agreements signals the interest of countries to systematise regulatory policy and co-operation. Further, the regulatory practices promoted by these horizontal chapters are strongly aligned with the 2012 Recommendation and the APEC-OECD Checklist, which supports consistency in approaches across jurisdictions.

These standalone chapters consistently advance regulatory impact assessment, stakeholder engagement and consideration of international standards. Yet, notably, a number of them go further and expand into new GRPs included in the 2012 Recommendation and recent OECD work, such as *ex post* evaluation, regulatory oversight and co-operation on regulatory enforcement.

These chapters build on and aim to complement existing rulemaking practices in trading partners. A majority of them create standing committees to monitor their implementation and/or promote regulatory co-operation among parties. While it is still early to assess their effects, these new bodies provide an opportunity to bring together relevant players working on improving regulatory effectiveness across policy communities.

The role of international organisations in IRC

International organisations (IOs) provide for an opportunity to co-operate on a larger scale than the bilateral approaches to IRC. They have been the main institutional form used to underpin multilateral regulatory co-operation for the past century [(OECD, 2013[11]) and (OECD, 2016[28])]. They offer platforms for continuous dialogue on and anticipation of new issues; help establish a common language; facilitate the comparability of approaches and practices; develop international instruments; and offer resolution mechanisms in case of disputes. They may take different forms: international, regional, groups of like-minded institutions or sharing common issues and priorities.

The international rulemaking landscape is dynamic with multiple actors and a fast-growing body of international instruments. It has evolved significantly over the years to accommodate new actors and forms of IOs. (OECD, 2016[28]) and (OECD, 2019[30]) classify the diverse international rule-makers in three broad categories: inter-governmental organisations (IGOs), trans-governmental networks (TGNs) and private standard-setting organisations. However, despite differences in nature, membership, mandate and focus, IOs share strong common features in developing and maintaining the body of international rules and standards: the pursuit of consensus in decision-making; the extension of traditional membership to new geographic zones and non-governmental actors; and the roles of their secretariat as information hubs.

IOs adopt a wide variety of international instruments with external normative value, which can be classified in several families with various attributes including legal stringency (OECD, 2019[30]). Nevertheless, international rulemaking functions largely as a system and not just a collection of actors and rules. Instruments serve as building blocks of a broader framework aimed at "regulating" specific areas. The vast ecosystem of IOs and rules is both a reflection of and a response to the increasing complexity of the modern world, the large number of issues requiring an international response and the variety of constituencies and situations. De facto, countries belong to 50 international organisations or more (OECD, 2013[11]). Evidence from (OECD, 2016[28]) shows that the international organisations who participated in the report had produced some 70 000 international instruments spanning a broad range of policy sectors.

But, with increasing complexity may come a perception of duplication, over-bureaucracy, inaccessibility, lack of transparency and accountability, weak implementation and loss of control. IOs are not immune from a context where trust in public institutions, evidence, and expert advice is deteriorating across all countries. In this context there is a need to improve the transparency, relevance and consistency of international rulemaking and ensure that it works as intended: as an instrument for managing globalisation for the well-being of all. With this objective in mind, the Partnership of International Organisations for Effective International Rulemaking aims to support IOs and their constituencies to address weaknesses in the implementation of international rules; promote evidence-based and transparent rulemaking; and encourage greater co-ordination among international rule makers.

Countries/domestic policy makers have a key role to play to ensure the quality of international rulemaking, through their active participation in international organisations, implementation of international instruments in domestic frameworks and role as relay of information on use and impacts of these instruments. This role is investigated in the Review of International Regulatory Co-operation of Mexico (OECD, 2018[41]) and the Review of International Regulatory Co-operation of the United Kingdom (OECD, 2016[28]).

Notes

[1] The wealth of co-operation mechanisms across regulators from different countries was highlighted in the detailed reviews of international regulatory co-operation carried out in Mexico and in the UK and provide practical examples of the binding and non-binding undertakings that may link them (OECD, 2018[41]) and (OECD, 2016[28]).

[2] In particular the development of an IRC toolkit by New Zealand.

[3] The latest is available at: https://www.pc.gov.au/inquiries/completed/mutual-recognition-schemes#report.

References

APEC-OECD (2005), *APEC-OECD Integrated Checklist on Regulatory Reform*, https://www.oecd.org/regreform/34989455.pdf.   [39]

Blanchard, O. (2017), *Macroeconomics*, Pearson, https://www.pearson.com/us/higher-education/program/blanchard-macroeconomics-7th-edition/pgm333935.html (accessed on 3 June 2021).   [17]

Correia de Brito, A., C. Kauffmann and J. Pelkmans (2016), "The contribution of mutual recognition to international regulatory co-operation", *OECD Regulatory Policy Working Papers*, No. 2, OECD Publishing, Paris, https://dx.doi.org/10.1787/5jm56fqsfxmx-en.   [40]

Giordani, P., M. Ruta and L. Zhu (2017), "Capital flow deflection", *Journal of International Economics*, pp. 102-118.   [15]

Gori, F., E. Lepers and C. Mehigan (2020), *Capital flow deflection under the magnifying glass*, OECD Publishing, Paris, https://dx.doi.org/10.1787/398180d0-en.   [16]

IFAC/BIAC (2018), *Regulatory Divergence: Costs, Risks, Impacts*, [25]
https://www.ifac.org/system/files/publications/files/IFAC-OECD-Regulatory-Divergence.pdf.

ITF (2019), *ITF Transport Outlook 2019*, OECD Publishing, Paris, [7]
https://dx.doi.org/10.1787/transp_outlook-en-2019-en.

Jeanne, O. (2014), *Macroprudential Policies in a Global Perspective*, National Bureau of [18]
Economic Research, http://dx.doi.org/10.3386/w19967.

Kauffmann, C. and R. Basedow (2016), "The political economy of international co-operation – a [29]
theoretical framework to understand international regulatory co-operation (IRC)", OECD,
Paris, unpublished working paper.

Kauffmann, C. and C. Saffirio (2021), "Good regulatory practices and co-operation in trade [34]
agreements: A historical perspective and stocktaking", *OECD Regulatory Policy Working
Papers*, No. 14, OECD Publishing, Paris, https://dx.doi.org/10.1787/cf520646-en.

Kauffmann, C. and C. Saffirio (2020), "Study of International Regulatory Co-operation (IRC) [21]
arrangements for air quality: The cases of the Convention on Long-Range Transboundary Air
Pollution, the Canada-United States Air Quality Agreement, and co-operation in North East
Asia", *OECD Regulatory Policy Working Papers*, No. 12, OECD Publishing, Paris,
https://dx.doi.org/10.1787/dc34d5e3-en.

OECD (2020), "No policy maker is an island: The international regulatory co-operation response [1]
to the COVID-19 crisis", OECD, Paris, http://www.oecd.org/coronavirus/policy-responses/no-
policy-maker-is-an-island-the-international-regulatory-co-operation-response-to-the-covid-19-
crisis-3011ccd0/ (accessed on 10 July 2020).

OECD (2020), *OECD Code of Liberalisation of Capital Movements*, [20]
http://www.oecd.org/investment/codes.htm (accessed on 20 March 2021).

OECD (2020), *OECD Study on the World Organisation for Animal Health (OIE) [22]
Observatory: Strengthening the Implementation of International Standards*, OECD Publishing,
Paris, https://dx.doi.org/10.1787/c88edbcd-en.

OECD (2019), *An Introduction to Online Platforms and Their Role in the Digital Transformation*, [9]
OECD Publishing, Paris, https://dx.doi.org/10.1787/53e5f593-en.

OECD (2019), *Challenges to Consumer Policy in the Digital Age: Background Report*, [4]
https://www.oecd.org/sti/consumer/challenges-to-consumer-policy-in-the-digital-age.pdf
(accessed on 3 March 2020).

OECD (2019), *International Migration Outlook 2019*, OECD Publishing, Paris, [5]
https://dx.doi.org/10.1787/c3e35eec-en.

OECD (2019), *Saving Costs in Chemicals Management: How the OECD Ensures Benefits to [27]
Society*, OECD Publishing, Paris, https://dx.doi.org/10.1787/9789264311718-en.

OECD (2019), *The Contribution of International Organisations to a Rule-Based International [38]
System*, OECD, Paris, https://www.oecd.org/gov/regulatory-policy/IO-Rule-
Based%20System.pdf.

OECD (2019), *The Contribution of International Organisations to a Rule-Based International System: Key Results from the Partnership of International Organisations for Effective Rulemaking*, https://www.oecd.org/gov/regulatory-policy/IO-Rule-Based%20System.pdf. [30]

OECD (2018), *Review of International Regulatory Co-operation of Mexico*, OECD Publishing, Paris, https://dx.doi.org/10.1787/9789264305748-en. [41]

OECD (2018), *The Resilience of Students with an Immigrant Background: Factors that Shape Well-being*, OECD Reviews of Migrant Education, OECD Publishing, Paris, https://dx.doi.org/10.1787/9789264292093-en. [6]

OECD (2017), *International Regulatory Co-operation and Trade: Understanding the Trade Costs of Regulatory Divergence and the Remedies*, OECD Publishing, Paris, https://dx.doi.org/10.1787/9789264275942-en. [24]

OECD (2017), *OECD Digital Economy Outlook 2017*, OECD Publishing, Paris, https://dx.doi.org/10.1787/9789264276284-en. [2]

OECD (2016), "Economic and Social Benefits of Internet Openness", *OECD Digital Economy Papers*, No. 257, OECD Publishing, Paris, https://dx.doi.org/10.1787/5jlwqf2r97g5-en. [8]

OECD (2016), *International Regulatory Co-operation: The Role of International Organisations in Fostering Better Rules of Globalisation*, OECD Publishing, Paris, https://dx.doi.org/10.1787/9789264244047-en. [28]

OECD (2015), *OECD Regulatory Policy Outlook 2015*, OECD Publishing, http://www.oecd-ilibrary.org/governance/oecd-regulatory-policy-outlook-2015_9789264238770-en. [37]

OECD (2013), *Interconnected Economies: Benefiting from Global Value Chains*, OECD Publishing, Paris, https://dx.doi.org/10.1787/9789264189560-en. [3]

OECD (2013), *International Regulatory Co-operation: Case Studies, Vol. 1: Chemicals, Consumer Products, Tax and Competition*, OECD Publishing, Paris, https://dx.doi.org/10.1787/9789264200487-en. [13]

OECD (2013), *International Regulatory Co-operation: Case Studies, Vol. 2: Canada-US Co-operation, EU Energy Regulation, Risk Assessment and Banking Supervision*, OECD Publishing, Paris, https://dx.doi.org/10.1787/9789264200500-en. [31]

OECD (2013), *International Regulatory Co-operation: Case Studies, Vol. 3: Transnational Private Regulation and Water Management*, OECD Publishing, Paris, https://dx.doi.org/10.1787/9789264200524-en. [23]

OECD (2013), *International Regulatory Co-operation: Addressing Global Challenges*, OECD Publishing, Paris, https://dx.doi.org/10.1787/9789264200463-en. [11]

OECD (2012), *Recommendation of the Council on Regulatory Policy and Governance*, http://www.oecd.org/gov/regulatory-policy/2012-recommendation.htm (accessed on 14 March 2019). [35]

OECD (2010), *Policy Framework for Effective and Efficient Financial Regulation*, OECD Publishing, Paris, http://www.oecd.org/daf/fin (accessed on 19 March 2021). [26]

OECD (1994), *Regulatory Co-operation for an Interdependent World*, Public Management   [10]
Studies, OECD Publishing, Paris, https://dx.doi.org/10.1787/9789264062436-en.

OECD (Forthcoming), *Implementation Toolkit on Legislative Actions for Consumer Protection*   [33]
Enforcement Co-operation.

OECD/ICN (2021), *OECD/ICN Report on International Co-operation in Competition*   [32]
Enforcement, http://www.oecd.org/daf/competition/oecd-icn-report-on-international-co-
operation-in-competition-enforcement.pdf.

OECD/WHO (2016), *International Regulatory Co-operation and International Organisations The*   [12]
Case of the World Health Organization (WHO).

OECD/WTO (2019), *Facilitating Trade through Regulatory Cooperation: The Case of the WTO's*   [36]
TBT/SPS Agreements and Committees, OECD Publishing, Paris/World Trade Organization,
Geneva, https://dx.doi.org/10.1787/ad3c655f-en.

Pasricha, G. et al. (2018), *Domestic and Multilateral Effects of Capital Controls in Emerging*   [14]
Markets, National Bureau of Economic Research, Cambridge, MA,
http://dx.doi.org/10.3386/w20822.

Pereira Da Silva, L. and M. Chui (2017), "Avoiding "regulatory wars" using international   [19]
coordination of macroprudential policies", https://www.bis.org/speeches/sp171003.pdf.

2 Best Practice Principles on International Regulatory Co-operation

This chapter sets the Best Practice Principles on International Regulatory Co-operation, helping guide regulators and policy makers in making systematic use of international regulatory co-operation. They are organised around three building blocks: Establishing the IRC strategy and its governance, embedding IRC throughout the domestic rulemaking and co-operating internationally (bilaterally, plurilaterally and multilaterally). Ultimately, these principles will support governments in operating a paradigm shift to adapt laws and regulations to an interconnected world.

The 2012 Recommendation on Regulatory Policy and Governance [OECD/LEGAL/0390] (the 2012 Recommendation) recognises that policy makers and regulators can no longer work in isolation. They have much to learn from their peers abroad, and much to benefit from pooling scarce resources and aligning approaches. IRC has become an essential building block to ensure the quality and relevance of regulation today. The 2012 Recommendation therefore encourages Members and non-Members having adhered to it (the Adherents) to "*In developing regulatory measures, give consideration to all relevant international standards and frameworks for co-operation in the same field and, where appropriate, their likely effects on parties outside the jurisdiction*" (Principle 12).

These *Best Practice Principles on International Regulatory Co-operation* (Best Practice Principle) support the implementation of Principle 12 of the 2012 Recommendation by offering general guidance rather than detailed prescription. Nevertheless, Best Practice Principles are intentionally ambitious. Few countries meet the principles highlighted below. It is nevertheless worth pointing that because it is scarcely used systematically, it does not mean that IRC is not achievable. On the contrary, there are a number of practices and approaches that are easy to adopt, notably as part of regulatory practices. In this perspective, these Principles aim to provide policy-makers and civil servants in both OECD member and partner countries with a practical instrument to make better use of IRC.

The Best Practice Principles are organised around three building blocks:

1. Establishing the IRC strategy and its governance;
2. Embedding IRC throughout the domestic rulemaking; and
3. Co-operating internationally (bilaterally, plurilaterally and multilaterally).

The Best Practice Principles are summarised in Box 2.1 and detailed below. Throughout the text, Boxes provide illustrations of existing practices to facilitate the understanding of the Best Practice Principles. However, this is an area under fast development and where more practices will emerge over time. The forthcoming APEC-OECD IRC Resource will provide concrete examples of IRC practices implemented by countries.

Box 2.1. Summary of the Best Practice Principles on International Regulatory Co- operation

Establishing the IRC strategy and its governance

- Develop a whole of government IRC policy / strategy
- Establish a co-ordination mechanism in government on IRC activities to centralise relevant information on IRC practices and activities and to build a consensus and common language
- Enable an IRC conducive framework – i.e. raise awareness of IRC, build on existing platforms for co-operation, reduce anti-IRC biases and build in incentives for policy makers and regulators

Embedding IRC throughout the domestic rulemaking

- Gather and rely on international knowledge and expertise
- Consider existing international instruments when developing regulation and document the rationale for departing from them
- Assess impacts beyond borders
- Engage actively with foreign stakeholders
- Embed consistency with international instruments as a key principle driving the review process in *ex post* evaluation and stock reviews

---

- Assess *ex ante* the co-operation needs to ensure appropriate enforcement and streamline "recognisable" procedures

Co-operating internationally (bilaterally, plurilaterally and multilaterally)

- Co-operate with other countries to promote the development and diffusion of good practices and innovations in regulatory policy and governance
- Contribute to international fora which support regulatory co-operation
- Use mutual recognition in combination with international instruments
- Align IRC expectations across various policy instruments, including in trade agreements

Establishing the IRC strategy and its governance

In many cases, more systematic consideration of the international environment in domestic rulemaking requires a significant change in the regulatory culture of countries. Given the dynamic and interconnected environment, this change consists in understanding and embedding a "beyond the border" perspective in rulemaking and establishing relevant regulatory co-operation across borders. Such a cultural shift requires dedicated attention to establishing a whole of government strategy for IRC and to its governance, including reviewing the extent to which the current institutional, legal and policy regulatory environment provides sufficient directions, guidance and incentives for IRC. It is worth noting that a solid regulatory policy framework, including effective oversight mechanisms, is a *sine qua non* condition for a jurisdiction to establish ambitious IRC.

Develop a whole of government IRC policy/strategy

An IRC policy can be defined as a systematic, national-level, whole-of-government policy/strategy promoting international regulatory co-operation whether reflected in a broad strategic document or other instrument. It may incorporate but goes beyond any specific agreement drawn with key partners or regional approach adopted to promote regulatory co-operation. This policy is an opportunity to convey political leadership and build a holistic IRC vision and strategy with clearly defined roles and responsibilities. It can also help set a definition on IRC, to support a common understanding across the government. Ultimately, the IRC policy is also important to ensure IRC practices of policymakers and regulators feed into the broader strategic priorities of the government. IRC being a core component of regulatory quality, an IRC policy needs not stand alone and can be fully integrated into a broader regulatory policy. Examples of such policies are still rare. Box 2.2 presents selected country examples.

Box 2.2. Selected examples of whole of Government strategy and policy frameworks for IRC

IRC is formally embedded in **Canada**'s overarching regulatory policy framework, the Cabinet Directive on Regulation (CDR). The CDR requires regulators to assess opportunities for co-operation and alignment with other jurisdictions, domestically and internationally, in order to reduce unnecessary regulatory burden on Canadian businesses while maintaining or improving the health, safety, security, social and economic well-being of Canadians, and protecting the environment.

The Treasury Board Secretariat (TBS), central oversight body in Canada has a team of 16 full-time employees responsible for supporting and co-ordinating efforts to foster international and domestic regulatory co-operation. This team works with regulators to ensure that they meet their obligations under the CDR and lead Canada's participation in different regulatory co-operation fora. TBS also

---

works closely with Global Affairs Canada to negotiate regulatory provisions in trade agreements, including those related to IRC.

In **New Zealand**, IRC considerations are embedded in core documents, including the Government Expectations for Good Regulatory Practice and the Government's Regulatory Management Strategy. Responsibility for oversight and promoting consideration of IRC is shared across several agencies: the Treasury's lead agency on good regulatory practice; the Ministry of Business, Innovation and Employment (MBIE), takes the lead on promoting international regulatory coherence, and the Ministry of Foreign Affairs and Trade which acts as lead advisor and negotiator on trade policy and provides advice on the process for entering into international treaties. The three authorities co-ordinate on different IRC areas: e.g on cross-cutting GRP and regulatory co-operation chapters in FTAs, representing New Zealand at international regulatory policy fora, and on contribution to benchmarking studies of regulation and the regulatory environment.

Sources: (OECD, 2018[1]) (OECD, 2016[2]).

While trade is a strong driver for IRC, an effective IRC narrative should go beyond the expected trade benefits. IRC has important broader benefits for policy makers, regulators and society across policy areas, for example via learning from foreign peers, or aligning approaches on common and cross-border policy challenges to strengthen the effectiveness of domestic regulation in achieving its policy objectives. Co-operation is also a cornerstone of effective market surveillance and regulatory enforcement. With the growing dematerialisation of flows transcending borders, regulatory co-operation across different jurisdictions is becoming critical to the identification of non-compliant behaviours, the detection of dangerous products and conducts and their remedies. From this perspective, IRC may help achieve other broader objectives such as safety, social and environmental.

The IRC policy/strategy should be evidence-based and acknowledge the key drivers, benefits, costs and challenges of co-operation. It should give priority to key partners for collaboration, taking into account the country's "dependence" on other countries (subject to sectors and / or policy areas) and account for IRC drivers and political economy. Typical IRC drivers include geographical proximity, economic interdependence, political and economic properties of potential partners (including relative size) and their like-mindedness, the maturity and proximity of the regulatory system, and the nature of regulation.

The IRC policy/strategy should account for the variety of IRC approaches. Different IRC approaches have different benefits and costs and may be more or less relevant depending on the sector/area under consideration. As their experience with IRC matures, policy makers should undertake more systematic *ex ante* and *ex post* assessment of their regulatory co-operation initiatives. They should develop a base of evidence on uses and impacts, relying on information collected via regulatory impacts assessment, *ex post* evaluation and data provided by international fora. This would help governments in updating the IRC policy/strategy over time based on evidence.

The IRC policy/strategy should also recognise that a level of unilateral adoption of international or of other jurisdictions' instruments may be warranted in sectors or policy areas where a country has accumulated less knowledge and expertise or where the country's limited activity may not warrant the necessary resources to develop its own approach. Opting to unilaterally recognise or uphold regulatory requirements issued by competent authorities in other jurisdictions can also be a flexible and rapid option for countries that can prove particularly useful during a crisis to quickly increase the supply and availability of goods and services. This has proved an important mechanism in the midst of the COVID-19 crisis to facilitate the trade of critical medical products and protective equipment.

Establish a co-ordination mechanism in government on IRC activities to build a consensus and common understanding on IRC and capitalise on relevant information on IRC practices and activities

IRC is part and parcel of the regulatory policy agenda and an important building block of regulatory quality. Nevertheless, it entails an ambitious rethinking of traditional domestic rulemaking processes. To ensure IRC is interwoven within the regulatory process and helps contribute best to domestic strategic objectives, the design and establishment of an IRC strategy requires the commitment of the regulatory oversight bodies. Yet its successful implementation is a whole-of-government endeavour involving different actors. It also requires a significant change in the administrative culture. As such, there should be dedicated staff strongly connected to the regulatory policy agenda with sufficient resources and influence to ensure maximum mainstreaming in the rulemaking practices of departments and regulators (Box 2.2).

There should be an IRC policy overseen, at least in its regulatory quality dimension, by the regulatory oversight bodies and capacities established in line with the 2012 Recommendation. These bodies have a key role to play to ensure the mainstreaming of IRC considerations in rulemaking practices, in the development of relevant guidance and in their systematic check during scrutiny work.

To ensure that countries develop an IRC policy and strategy in line with those impacted (country specific policy making community, regulators, businesses, affected communities, etc.), and in line with core regulatory policy principles, the oversight unit should highlight in any IRC guidance the importance of transparency, such as systematic publication of IRC documents, and promote wide consultation on the overall IRC strategy or its components. Public availability of the IRC policy/strategy can support governments in ensuring transparency and accountability about international co-operation efforts.

The successful implementation of an IRC policy/strategy is a shared endeavour across government. The entity responsible for the IRC strategy should pro-actively promote it across government and ensure appropriate linkages with other, related, policies and initiatives across government (i.e. trade and foreign policy). Typically, Foreign Ministries and overseas embassies have a role to facilitate IRC by providing access to networks, stakeholder and information, and often by co-ordinating participation in international organisations.

Enable an IRC conducive framework – i.e. raise awareness of IRC, build on existing platforms for co-operation, reduce anti-IRC biases and build in incentives for policy makers and regulators

Existing legal and policy documents and guidance on regulatory policy may generate obstacles for regulators to consider more systematically the international environment and engage in fruitful IRC. Updating these documents may help remove some of the unintended biases, embed stronger IRC incentive, and reduce legal and institutional impediments to co-operation. As an example, in 2018, Canada introduced amendments to the Red Tape Reduction Act to allow regulators to count reductions in administrative burden to businesses that occur in other jurisdictions as part of their one for one mechanism, should they result from a work plan under one of Canada's three formal regulatory co-operation tables.

In addition, guidance to regulators should incorporate IRC elements and guide regulators on how to embed IRC in regulatory management tools (see below). For example, such guidance could clarify the standard of international evidence to be used in the RIA process and help regulators identify the applicable international instruments. While such a standard is still to be developed and could be the object of further OECD work, relevant information to be collected by regulators include data from other jurisdictions and international fora on the challenges they seek to address (i.e. patterns, evolution over time, impacts on various populations, among other), and on policies, their use and impacts in other jurisdictions. There is a wide range of information sources that can be tapped on, including official government data, international organisations, peer reviewed academic work.

Regulators at various levels of governance know best what co-operation mechanisms exist in their own area. Nevertheless, there is an opportunity for national levels to support and leverage existing regulators fora and build a community of IRC practices and other regulatory policy topics, raise awareness about IRC tools, and identify training needs when relevant (Box 2.3).

Box 2.3. Communities of regulatory practices

Canada's Community of Federal Regulators (CFR) is a partnership of Canadian regulatory organisations at the federal level that aims to facilitate professional development, collaboration and advancement of the regulatory field. The community serves approximately 40 000 regulatory professionals who support Canada's regulatory lifecycle. The community is governed by a Deputy Minister Champion, two Assistant Deputy Minister Co-Champions and representatives from each of the departments and agencies providing financial support to the community, responsible for setting direction and areas of focus for the community in conjunction with the CFR Office. The CFR has an awards system which incentivises IRC through a specific category to Excellence in Regulatory Co-operation & Collaboration. This award recognises a regulatory initiative that has demonstrated success through a collaborative or co-operative endeavour with another organisation and/or jurisdiction.

New Zealand Government Regulatory Practice Initiative (G-REG) is a network of central and local government regulatory agencies established to lead and contribute to regulatory practice initiatives. G-REG focuses on developing people capability, organisational capability, and building a professional community of regulators. It is a network for all regulators in the public sector, whether at central or local government.

The Chair in Regulatory Practice enables international regulatory best practice and knowledge to be disseminated to G-REG and the wider regulatory community (through blogs, seminars and guest lectures), so New Zealand can learn from the rest of the world. G-REG's peer learning framework incorporates an international element by, among other things, focusing on the need to minimise the potential for unintended negative impacts of regulatory activities on regulated entities or affected supplier industries and supply chains, which are often international or regional.

Sources: (OECD, 2018[1]) (OECD, 2016[2]).

Embedding IRC throughout the domestic rulemaking

IRC has important implications for the activities of regulators and of their oversight bodies. It requires a change in the regulatory culture towards greater consideration of the international environment in the rule-making process. This involves the more systematic review and consideration of foreign and international regulatory frameworks of relevance when regulating and the assessment of how regulatory measures impact and fit within the broader cross-border management of the issue to address. There is a need to consider IRC in all phases of the rulemaking cycle, from the initiation of new laws and regulations to their implementation, evaluation and revision. In this perspective, the regulatory management tools (Regulatory Impact Assessment, stakeholder engagement and *ex post* reviews of regulation) provide important entry points in the rule-making process to consider the international environment in the development and revision of laws and regulations.

Gather and rely on international knowledge and expertise

At a minimum, Governments should act in accordance with their international treaty obligations, which infers appropriate co-ordination across government and a clear information base on such commitments.

In developing laws and regulation, policy makers and regulators should gather evidence and expertise that may go beyond their own jurisdiction. It is rare that a new issue arises without any other jurisdiction and international organisation having had to deal with it. Gathering the intelligence around the incidence of the issue at stake and the approaches adopted by others can help build the body of evidence on the area under consideration, identify a greater range of options for action, and develop the narrative around the chosen measure. This can be done as part of the routine practice of gathering information during *ex ante* RIAs and *ex post* evaluations. It can also be done by engaging with relevant experts and public and private sector representatives and practitioners from around the world, complementing traditional stakeholder engagement (see below). For example, Turkey's 11th Development Plan (2019-2023) includes a section on National Capacity for International Cooperation that calls for exchanges with experts from other countries for the preparation of legislation dealing with regulating financial and technical issues (Presidency of the Republic of Turkey, 2019[3]).

Consider existing international instruments when developing regulation and document the rationale for departing from them

International normative instruments are usually the results of significant evidence gathering and consensus building (including scientific). Using them in domestic legislation provides a strong driver for regulatory consistency internationally therefore reducing the opportunities for arbitrage and the costs for the regulated entities of having to comply with multiple requirements. Binding instruments should be embodied in domestic law and regulations depending on the process set out to that effect. With regard to non-binding instruments, they should be taken into account and, when specific circumstances require departing from them, this should be justified based on evidence. For examples of domestic requirements to consider international instruments, see Box 2.4. Traditional regulatory management tools such as RIA or stakeholder engagement can help in the assessment of the benefits and costs of pursuing a unilateral approach versus relying on an existing international solution.

The principle of use of relevant international standards is already strongly embedded in the WTO SPS and TBT agreements from a trade impact perspective. Indeed, the use of international technical standards is particularly relevant in the development of domestic standards, technical regulations and conformity assessment procedures (sometimes referred to as STRACAP) to facilitate trade. Nevertheless, the use of relevant international instruments merits to be extended beyond the technical standard area and to apply more broadly. Indeed, in areas not directly related to trade, use of international instruments in decision making and the harmonisation of international approaches allow to avoid free riding behaviour and limit costs on businesses and citizens – this is typically the case in the tax area or corruption. Such a principle is valid for all jurisdictions but hold particularly true for those that have directly contributed to the development of such instruments.

For maximum interoperability gains, incorporation by reference of international instruments[1] should be the preferred option when legally feasible. However, its limited use so far may well reflect a perceived lack of appropriateness of international instruments to specific country situations and the limited confidence of domestic regulators that these instruments may (without alteration) help them achieve their policy objectives. Hence this principle goes hand in hand with the need for policy makers and regulators to actively participate in international fora where such instruments are being developed (see below).

The 2018 *Regulatory Policy Outlook* highlights the importance of facilitating the access to applicable international instruments, whether legally binding or not, through centralised databases (by sector/policy areas or other) (OECD, 2018[4]).

Box 2.4. Embedding international instruments in domestic regulation

In **Australia**, there is a cross-sectoral requirement to consider "consistency with Australia's international obligations and relevant international accepted standards and practices" (COAG Best Practice Regulation). Wherever possible, regulatory measures or standards are required to be compatible with relevant international or internationally accepted standards or practices in order to minimise impediments to trade. If a regulatory option involves establishing or amending standards in areas where international standards already apply, the proponent should document whether (and why) the proposed standards differ from the international standard.

Mexico has various provisions encouraging the adoption of international standards, mostly bearing on technical regulations and standards. If international standards do not exist, the consideration of foreign standards is encouraged, in particular standards of two major trading partners, the United States and the EU. To support regulators in this obligation, a guidance document on how to embed international standards in domestic technical regulations or standards was developed, and some examples of international and foreign standards are listed in the legal obligation.

The **New Zealand** Government Expectations for Good Regulatory Practice apply to all New Zealand's regulatory systems and therefore to all kinds of regulatory measures and actors. This provides that "the government believes that durable outcomes of real value to New Zealanders are more likely when a regulatory system … is consistent with relevant international standards and practices to maximise the benefits from trade and from cross border flows of people, capital and ideas (except when this would compromise important domestic objectives and values)". Regulatory agencies are expected to undertake "systematic impact and risk analysis, including assessing alternative legislative and non-legislative policy options, and how the proposed change might interact or align with existing domestic and international requirements within this or related regulatory systems".

In the **United States**, the guidance of the Office of Management and Budget (OMB) on the use of voluntary consensus standards states that "in the interests of promoting trade and implementing the provisions of international treaty agreements, your agency should consider international standards in procurement and regulatory applications". In addition, the Executive Order 13609 on Promoting International Regulatory Co-operation states that agencies shall, "for significant regulations that the agency identifies as having significant international impacts, consider, to the extent feasible, appropriate, and consistent with law, any regulatory approaches by a foreign government that the United States has agreed to consider under a regulatory cooperation council work plan." The scope of this requirement is limited to the sectoral work plans that the United States has agreed to in Regulatory Cooperation Councils. The scope of this requirement is limited to the sectoral work plans that the United States has agreed to in Regulatory Cooperation Councils.

Source: (OECD, 2018[11]) (OECD, 2016[2]).

Assess impacts beyond borders

At a minimum, governments should ensure that their rulemaking takes into account the potential impacts on parties outside of the national boundaries. The Regulatory Impact Assessment process provides an opportunity to do so, in particular through the assessment of trade impacts and of impacts on foreign jurisdictions. But while countries have started accounting for the trade impacts of their rulemaking (Box 2.5), the broader consideration of impacts of their regulatory action beyond their own borders (and potentially therefore of the second round effects) remains limited. To be effectively implemented, this principle goes hand in hand with the need to provide opportunities for consultation with external partners on the development of regulation (see below).

Box 2.5. Assessing Trade Impacts through Regulatory Impact Assessment Procedures

- **Review of International Regulatory Co-operation of Mexico** (OECD, 2018[1]): Mexico introduced a trade filter in the RIA process that provides an opportunity to assess the impacts on exports and imports of a regulatory measure and triggers the involvement of the Trade Ministry for notification to WTO. Through nine detailed questions, this trade filter allows regulators to identify potential trade impacts of draft regulations. If such an impact is found, a specific trade RIA is conducted and the draft measure is notified to the WTO, thus opening the possibility to gather feedback on the measure from other WTO members and potentially stakeholders therein.

- **Review of International Regulatory Co-operation of the United Kingdom** (OECD, 2016[2]): the UK introduced a new RIA template in 2018, including a new question related to the impacts of UK regulations on international trade and investment (i.e. *Is this measure likely to impact on trade and investment? Yes/No*). This new template was trialled in 2019. Based on the first set of responses to this template, the UK Department of International Trade, Better Regulation Executive and Regulatory Policy Committee are working together on how to refine the methodologies to support departments in measuring the trade impacts of their draft measures.

Source: (OECD, 2018[1]) (OECD, 2016[2]).

Engage actively with foreign stakeholders

Engagement of foreign stakeholders in regulatory processes – as an integral part of regular stakeholder engagement most commonly focused on domestic actors – can help raise awareness for regulatory approaches in other jurisdictions and provide information on enforcement consequences of selected regulatory options, including their impacts on trade and the practical effects of maintaining the same or different regulatory approaches. In practice, it is necessary but not sufficient to rely on open, non-discriminatory engagement processes domestically, for example via open-access internet platforms accessible to all. Countries should make an extra effort to involve foreign stakeholders. This can take the form of specific communication through business platforms or chambers of commerce.

Compulsory notification of draft regulations to international fora provides an important means by which to alert and draw inputs from foreign stakeholders. The WTO TBT and SPS Agreements provide such opportunity through the single central government authority responsible for notifications (OECD/WTO, 2019[5]) (Karttunen, 2020[6]). However, other notification processes exist in various sectors and regional platforms, such as for example notification obligations of environmental impact assessments under the UNECE's Convention on Environmental Impact Assessment in a Transboundary Context (Espoo Convention) (Kauffmann and Saffirio, 2020[7]). Such notification processes can usefully complement the mechanisms established by regulatory oversight bodies and need to feed in and work in synch with those mechanisms.

Embed consistency with international instruments as a key principle driving the review process in ex post *evaluation and stock reviews*

The full extent of the impacts of a regulatory measure is only known after its implementation. Therefore, *ex post* evaluation provides a critical opportunity to identify regulatory divergences with international frameworks as well as their trade and other potential impacts. Evaluation and stock reviews can be used more systematically to map the state of international knowledge on the regulated area and take stock of new approaches adopted by other jurisdictions that may have proved successful. It should analyse the costs (and benefits) of diverging from international practice if such a choice was made *ex ante* and identify the unintended divergences (in design and enforcement) that may be source of frictions (Box 2.6).

Given the potential relevance of the findings of such *ex post* evaluation for other jurisdictions and the international community, the results of *ex post* evaluation should be made public and available to relevant partners and international fora to the extent possible.

Box 2.6. Evaluations and stock reviews as opportunities to identify divergences internationally and gather new intelligence

In the updated version of **Canada**'s Directive on Regulation regulators must, as part of stock reviews, identify new opportunities to reduce regulatory burdens on stakeholders through regulatory co-operation activities

In **New Zealand**, regulatory agencies are expected to "periodically look at other similar regulatory systems, in New Zealand and other jurisdictions, for possible trends, threats, linkages, opportunities for alignment, economies of scale and scope, and examples of innovation and good practice".

Source: (OECD, 2018[1]) (OECD, 2016[2]).

Assess* ex ante *the co-operation needs to ensure appropriate enforcement and streamline "recognisable" procedures

Given the impacts of digitalisation and the fragmentation of value chains, it is likely that appropriate enforcement of any rule will require co-ordination with foreign jurisdictions, be it to gather relevant information on the market structure or to solve cases or find remediation when applicable enforcement authority or mechanism is located outside of the jurisdiction. Such enforcement co-operation needs are better estimated and foreseen early in the rule-making process in order to avoid gaps in the applicability of rules. More broadly, enforcement co-operation can be facilitated by ensuring that regulators have the appropriate tools/ legal authority to co-operate and take action provided by their domestic legislation (OECD, Forthcoming[8]).

Conformity assessment procedures allow companies to demonstrate compliance with regulatory requirements. When the foundations of mutual recognition and equivalence mechanisms, they are a key element to facilitate international trade and provide confidence that traded goods and services are fit for purpose. However, when different and not recognised across countries, they can add substantial costs to traders and limit the flow of quality products. Improving their quality domestically and facilitating recognition of trustworthy partners' conformity assessment procedures can help regulators reduce their load domestically and limit compliance costs for regulated entities.

Co-operating internationally (bilaterally, plurilaterally & multilaterally)

Unilateral actions of countries to embed greater consideration of the international environment in domestic rulemaking and map and ensure greater consistency with relevant international frameworks provide essential building blocks of IRC. They help avoid the unnecessary regulatory divergences through better informed rulemaking and foster the mutual knowledge and confidence needed across jurisdictions. Stronger forms of bilateral, regional or international co-operation approaches are however needed (and de facto exist) to lay the ground of institutionalised and continuous collaboration and of greater coherence in regulatory matters. The modalities of international co-operation will depend on the legal and administrative system and geographic location of the country, as well as on the sector or policy area under consideration.

Co-operate with other countries to promote the development and diffusion of good practices and innovations in regulatory policy and governance

Good regulatory practices are the foundations of trustworthy regulatory institutions and frameworks. They are also the building blocks of stronger regulatory co-operation approaches and mechanisms. Countries should continue co-operating within the OECD and other relevant frameworks at a global scale to advance the knowledge and understanding of good regulatory practices, establish common language on key regulatory policy terms and concepts, and strengthen the confidence needed across jurisdictions for stronger forms of IRC. Co-operating internationally on good regulatory practices can be the opportunity for governments both to learn from others' experiences and to build capacity of other countries with less developed good regulatory practice frameworks.

Contribute to international fora which support regulatory co-operation

Governments are encouraged to participate plainly in international organisations where science is discussed, practices shared, and common approaches and international instruments developed. They are usually consensus based and provide an opportunity to both collect evidence and gather expertise on issues of common interest and influence international rulemaking. In this perspective, it may be useful for countries to build a comprehensive mapping of all the international organisations that they contribute to. Where resources may be limited, sharing the burden of active participation among likeminded countries may help address the capacity challenges. At a minimum, continuous surveillance of the normative activity of international organisations will help identify when issues of relevance to a specific jurisdiction are being raised.

Beyond the active participation in the technical work of international organisations, countries could further support the use of good regulatory practices at the international level. Through their membership or participation in technical committees, national jurisdictions have a role to play in sending consistent messages and working towards the development of more transparent, evidence based, co-ordinated rules and no more burdensome than necessary to achieve legitimate policy objectives. They can, in particular, support greater engagement of a wide variety of stakeholders (both national and international) in the normative activity of international organisations, more *ex ante* and *ex post* evaluation of international instruments, stronger implementation and co-ordination of joint rules. The work of the Partnership of International Organisations for Effective International Rulemaking, spearheaded by the RPC, aims to provide a unique reference base on the practical steps that international organisations can take in this direction (OECD, 2021 forthcoming[9]).

The 2018 *Regulatory Policy Outlook* identifies a disconnect between the domestic and the international rulemaking processes, which generates inefficiencies. Better use of regulatory management tools across domestic and international levels may help bridge this disconnect. For example, greater monitoring and more regular evaluation of the application of international instruments at domestic level would help make the case for their use and inform domestic regulators of their expected and realised impacts. It would also help inform the revision of international instruments if evaluation results were shared more systematically across levels of government.

Use mutual recognition in combination with international instruments

In areas where regulatory harmonisation may not be needed and it is recognised that various regulatory approaches may achieve similar objectives, the mutual (or even unilateral) recognition of the other jurisdiction's rules, conformity assessment procedures or enforcement results may avoid undue costs to business and enforcement clogging. Experience shows however that such recognition is most easily achieved among like-minded countries, and made less costly and facilitated by coherence and convergence in the underlying rules.

Align IRC expectations across various policy instruments, including trade agreements

Trade agreements are increasingly used as a mechanism to promote considerations on regulatory quality and co-operation. Most recently, a number of agreements incorporate standalone chapters focused on GRPs, IRC or both. These chapters can represent an important political commitment and serve to advance common understanding and use of regulatory co-operation and regulatory management tools across jurisdictions.

It is important though that consistency with the international commitments of countries in the same field is respected, in particular the 2012 Recommendation and the APEC-OECD Checklist. Where such standalone chapters create special standing bodies to oversee the implementation of these chapters and/or promote regulatory co-operation, countries should ensure that they effectively and efficiently deliver on their purpose avoiding overlaps with other bodies or the risk of co-operation fatigue. In particular, these bodies should provide an opportunity to bring together critical players working on improving regulatory effectiveness across policy communities in each country. An example is provided by the CETA (Box 2.7).

Box 2.7. The EU-Canada Comprehensive Economic and Trade Agreement (CETA)

The CETA, provisionally in force since September 2017, includes a mechanism to develop voluntary regulatory co-operation between the Parties, called the Regulatory Cooperation Forum (RCF). Co-operation in the framework of the RCF is voluntary and driven by the Parties' willingness to identify areas of common work, without prejudice to their ability to continue developing their own regulatory, legislative and policy initiatives.

The RCF facilitates regulatory co-operation between the Parties through its following functions:

- Provide a forum to discuss regulatory policy issues of mutual interest that the Parties have identified through, among others, consultations with interested stakeholders;
- Assist individual regulators to identify potential partners for co-operation activities;
- Review regulatory initiatives, whether in progress or anticipated, that a Party considers may provide potential for co-operation;
- Encourage the development of bilateral co-operation activities and, on the basis of information obtained from regulatory departments and agencies, review the progress and achievements and share the best practices of regulatory co-operation initiatives in specific sectors.

The RCF is co-chaired by EU and Canadian officials overseeing bilateral trade and regulatory co-operation. Although the RCF is set up as part of CETA, it also covers co-operation activities that are not directly related to trade between the Parties and that aim at enhancing administrative efficiency

---

and/or at tackling at bilateral level policy issues that transcend national or continental borders. Individual regulators co-operating under the framework of the RCF cover areas such as consumer protection, public health, digital economy or animal welfare.

To inform their regulatory co-operation activities, both Parties carried out consultations in 2018 in order to collect views of European and Canadian stakeholders for potential topics where EU and Canadian regulators could meaningfully co-operate. On this basis, five fields of co-operation were identified at the first meeting of the RCF in December 2018: i) cybersecurity and the internet of things; ii) animal welfare – transportation of animals; iii) re-testing of cosmetics-like products; iv) co-operation on pharmaceutical inspections in third countries; and v) exchange of information on the safety of consumer products; and a work plan adopted.

Source: (Kauffmann and Saffirio, 2021[10]).

Note

[1] Incorporation by reference refers to the incorporation of international instruments in domestic instruments by means of a reference to one or more international instruments, or the replacement of entire text in the drafting of a code or regulation (OECD, 2013[11]).

References

Karttunen, M. (2020), *Transparency in the WTO SPS and TBT Agreements*, Cambridge University Press, http://dx.doi.org/10.1017/9781108762946. [6]

Kauffmann, C. and C. Saffirio (2021), "Good regulatory practices and co-operation in trade agreements: A historical perspective and stocktaking", *OECD Regulatory Policy Working Papers*, No. 14, OECD Publishing, Paris, https://dx.doi.org/10.1787/cf520646-en. [10]

Kauffmann, C. and C. Saffirio (2020), "Study of International Regulatory Co-operation (IRC) arrangements for air quality: The cases of the Convention on Long-Range Transboundary Air Pollution, the Canada-United States Air Quality Agreement, and co-operation in North East Asia", *OECD Regulatory Policy Working Papers*, No. 12, OECD Publishing, Paris, https://dx.doi.org/10.1787/dc34d5e3-en. [7]

OECD (2018), *OECD Regulatory Policy Outlook 2018*, OECD Publishing, Paris, https://dx.doi.org/10.1787/9789264303072-en. [4]

OECD (2018), *Review of International Regulatory Co-operation of Mexico*, OECD Publishing, Paris, https://dx.doi.org/10.1787/9789264305748-en. [1]

OECD (2016), *International Regulatory Co-operation: The Role of International Organisations in Fostering Better Rules of Globalisation*, OECD Publishing, Paris, https://dx.doi.org/10.1787/9789264244047-en. [2]

OECD (2013), *International Regulatory Co-operation: Addressing Global Challenges*, OECD Publishing, Paris, https://dx.doi.org/10.1787/9789264200463-en. [11]

OECD (2021 forthcoming), "Compendium of International Organisations' Practices: Working Towards Effective International Rulemaking". [9]

OECD (Forthcoming), *Implementation Toolkit on Legislative Actions for Consumer Protection Enforcement Co-operation*. [8]

OECD/WTO (2019), *Facilitating Trade through Regulatory Cooperation: The Case of the WTO's TBT/SPS Agreements and Committees*, OECD Publishing, Paris/World Trade Organization, Geneva, https://dx.doi.org/10.1787/ad3c655f-en. [5]

Presidency of the Republic of Turkey (2019), *Eleventh Development Plan (2019-2023)*, https://www.sbb.gov.tr/wp-content/uploads/2020/03/On_BirinciPLan_ingilizce_SonBaski.pdf. [3]

Annex A. Synthesis of advantages and disadvantages of various forms of IRC

The OECD analytical work has identified a number of advantages and disadvantages that may materialise when countries make use of the different approaches to IRC. In particular (OECD, 2013[1]) identified four potential benefits (economic gains; progress in managing risks and externalities across borders; administrative efficiency; and knowledge flow) and four potential costs or obstacles to IRC (the costs of maintaining the co-operation, the flexibility to co-operate, the real or perceived loss of sovereignty; and the implementation bottlenecks). This annex summarises these benefits and challenges as in (OECD, 2013[1]), acknowledging that they do not take place systematically.

The benefits of IRC (OECD 2013)

The literature generally supports the view that regulatory co-operation leads to **economic gains** through reduced transaction costs and economies of scale. Regulatory convergence is expected to permit firms to "utilize standardized contracts, documents and procedures to achieve economies of scale, reduce search and transaction costs, and simplify bargaining" (Lazer, 2001[2]). Identical regulations should help reduce the cost of production by allowing companies to maintain single production processes, rather than multiple processes to accommodate for multiple standards regimes (Drezner, 2008[3]). The decrease in marginal costs for firms resulting from increased regulatory co-operation will in turn generate an increase in consumer surplus and social welfare (e.g. through greater product choice, lower prices, faster access to new products) (Abbott and Snidal, 2000[4]). Similarly, increased information sharing allowed by greater co-operation should lead to a decrease in domestic funds spent on duplicative scientific and policy research, freeing resources that in turn could be allocated to more efficient uses. Regulatory co-operation can improve market access and increase trade and investment flows. As noted by (Drezner, 2008[3]), "uncoordinated, disparate regulatory structures function as implicit barriers to trade".

Where externalities are of a global nature, regulators will not be able to address them from a pure domestic angle. Typically, the ability to adequately regulate industrial pollution, trade in hazardous chemicals, infectious diseases, climate change and effectively manage cross-border risks will require co-ordination across neighbouring countries to ensure **effectiveness of regulatory measures**. If not, the regulatory measures risk being misdirected, inefficient or not adapted. Without even mentioning the management of global goods, in today's global world, policies adopted in one jurisdiction are likely to have strong extra-territorial implications, to the extent that it may become almost impossible for certain national policy objectives to be achieved without careful consideration of the international context. According to (Esty and Geradin, 2000[5]), if regulators ignore impacts beyond their own jurisdiction the standards they set will be systematically suboptimal (too low if they overlook transboundary regulatory benefits and too high if they disregard transboundary regulatory costs). This may prompt regulators to co-operate in order to achieve national regulatory objectives that are strongly affected by freer movement of goods, services and people. In addition, regulatory co-operation may enhance compliance and reduce the risks of a race to the bottom, overall amplifying the impact of domestic regulation.

Work-sharing across governments and public authorities, in which countries co-operate to address similar problems, including at bilateral, regional and multilateral levels may lead to important **administrative cost savings** that allow countries to rationalise the context of their own regulatory programmes and reallocate scarce public resources to areas of higher priority. Regulatory co-operation "may exploit the commonality of issues facing regulators at all levels of government, reduce the "learning curve" with respect to new or emerging concerns, increase the speed and effectiveness of regulatory action on cross-border issues, and permit efficient use of scarce information and analytical resources" (OECD, 1994[6]). Greater transparency may also provide opportunities for more efficient administrative relations with other countries, for instance, through simplification and harmonisation of administrative procedures. The gains may be specific and measurable, or they may be achieved less directly, for instance, through better understanding of the complex interplay between multiple policy goals, which may facilitate national decision-making and policy co-ordination.

Transferring good regulatory practices is an important benefit of IRC. IRC facilitates the exchange of information on regulatory practices between countries with different policy experience the access to good practices, making it a capacity building tool. This result reflects the findings in the literature. (Meuwese, 2009[7]) for instance finds a convergence on norms of standard-setting and regulatory impact assessment through enhanced dialogue between the EU Commission and the US Office of Management and Budget. The horizontal dialogue has both learning (exchange of best practices) and facilitative (reducing trade obstacles and improve sector-specific regulation) aspects. Similarly, according to (Raustiala, 2002[8]), transgovernmental networks allow "regulatory export", i.e. the export of regulatory rules and practices, which promotes regulatory convergence across states through "network effects". This effect can help build bureaucratic capacity in weaker states, which, in turn, can improve domestic regulation and support regulatory co-operation.

The costs and challenges of IRC

Costs involve the direct **costs** of the co-ordination infrastructure, i.e. of the IGO, of the secretariat established to manage treaties, of the institution managing the network and of the co-ordinated action. In addition, there is a number of direct and indirect costs related to the development of the co-operation and any change in the domestic status quo that co-operation with other jurisdictions may require. The costs for the governments include the time and resources that must be invested in the necessary political capital to make legal and administrative reforms happen, to mobilise bureaucratic actors, to lobby legislatures, and to mollify interest groups. The indirect costs relate to private actors having to retool their operations in order to comply with new regulations.

Differences between countries in their regulatory procedures and/or legal systems or traditions may significantly complicate efforts to overcome regulatory divergence. In some cases, regulatory paths are already deeply entrenched making rapprochement difficult. If not insurmountable, lack of regulatory flexibility can be a substantial impediment to IRC. This can take several forms, ranging from differences in approaches to key regulatory concepts and issues, to variations in institutional set up that make the relationships unbalanced. Legal obstacles to information sharing are presented as recurrent obstacles to co-operation. Closely related, the confidentiality of business information remains an important bottleneck, with firms often reluctant to see their product information shared between governments at the pre-market review stage.

Significant hurdles often arise in cases where regulatory co-operation is seen as compromising the principle of **regulatory sovereignty** or as insufficiently tailored to the needs of a given State or region. Even the application of usually non-controversial procedures can in some cases become sensitive, if they are interpreted as compromising key national interests or values. A number of scholars focus on the impact of delegation of regulatory powers on accountability. (Howse, 2012[9]) for example highlights inherent issues of democratic deficits arising from a delegation of powers, which takes place when co-operative regulatory activity is authorised by constitutional representative institutions. Making regulatory co-operation more transparent would help solve this dilemma. However, this may come at the price of reduced effectiveness of regulatory co-operation because the common advantage of informal give-and-take in a climate of trust would be restricted. In practice, the debate on national preferences and the preservation of sovereignty can be a lively one. At the same time, in a number of IRC experiences, some loss of sovereignty and/or sharing of competences is perceived as being balanced by a stronger international position, i.e. the Nordic Cooperation, the Australia-New Zealand co-operation and the Benelux Union.

The **political economy of regulatory co-operation** like any co-operation agreement across states and other stakeholders is complex. A number of factors combine. According to (Lazer, 2001[2]), States may not harmonise because 1) they are battling over the gains of harmonisation; ii) the actual transaction of reaching a compromise is complex, or iii) political elites gain political rents from non-harmonisation. In some cases, the co-operation may collapse because it is deemed captured by specific interest and it loses its credibility. Co-operation will not be sustainable if it is not perceived as mutually beneficial to all participating countries. However, the costs and benefits of IRC may not be spread equally across countries, giving different incentives to partners to co-operate. Some of the benefits may also not be easily appropriable by countries and while IRC may be beneficial overall, countries may not factor in the global good. In addition, when countries work together, there is always the possibility of "free-riding", i.e. that some countries derive the benefits without incurring the cost of co-operating. This may typically happen in a number of environmental issues, including climate change for which the temptation of free-riding is significant and the burden of action does not fall equally on all, prompting discussions of compensation mechanisms.

Beyond the signing of agreements and the high level commitment to regulatory co-operation, concretely **implementing IRC may be strewn with obstacles**. This is an area where case studies are helpful to identify the concrete challenges that implementing IRC may generate. Challenges may be related to a difficult enforcement of the IRC agreement or to a lack of effectiveness of the agreement to achieve its objectives. According to (Levy, 2016[10]), the effectiveness of co-operative arrangements is in turn affected by two factors: on the one hand the comprehensiveness of coverage and, on the other hand, rule credibility. Rule credibility can be further broken down into: i) rule process legitimacy; ii) monitoring quality; iii) enforcement quality; and iv) monitoring and enforcement legitimacy.

The strengths and weaknesses of various IRC approaches

Beyond the generic benefits and challenges of IRC highlighted in the literature and identified above, each specific approach to IRC has strengths and weaknesses (Table A A.1).

Table A A.1. Advantages and disadvantages of various IRC forms

Type of mechanism	Advantages	Disadvantages
Integration / harmonisation	The rules are the same for all. Compliance is the greatest. Supranational modes of governance are less likely to regulatory capture than networked forms.	Long process. Costs of the structure and of enforcement. Extensive delegation may be perceived as threatening the popular legitimacy of the mechanism.
Regulatory partnerships between countries	High-level engagement provides a strong signal that supports greater co-operation at lower levels (between regulators). Evidence that such partnerships avoid race to the bottom type of effects. Co-operative agreement that provides a flexible mechanism to address necessary evolution in the partnership.	The federal-only nature of the regulatory initiatives may generate difficulty to address regulations at different levels of jurisdiction.
Intergovernmental organisations	Provide platforms to promote continuous dialogue and anticipate emerging issues. Laboratory of co-operation experiments, laying the groundwork for broader and legally binding international agreements.	May be perceived as talk shops where progress is slow to materialise. Some weaknesses in enforcement and compliance.
Regional agreements with regulatory provisions	Legal force and direct connection to trade and economic integration. Regional agreements offer deeper levels of integration and a higher degree of co-operation than bilateral agreements. They offer economies of scale in enforcement.	May lead to a proliferation of provisions with limited consistency.
Area-specific legally binding agreements	Legal force	Lack of enforcement in some cases. Bilateral agreements may not be sufficient to ensure proper co-operation where multilateral co-ordination is needed (tax matters).

Type of mechanism	Advantages	Disadvantages
MRA (mutual recognition agreements)	Preserve State sovereignty in rule making and induces minimal adjustment costs. Reduce duplication efforts. May constitute a useful precursor to harmonisation.	The time and cost required to negotiate MR agreements can be high. MRAs require broadly similar regimes and extensive trust between parties and discussions every time changes occur in regulations in one of the co-operating party. Lack of enforcement (some MRAs between the EU and the United States are not enforced). Robust mechanisms need to be established and maintained to deal with disputes.
Transgovernmental networks	Low-cost, flexible and adaptable / scalable structures, which foster experimentation and innovation. Network regulation supports trust building, technical approaches and may help avoid race to the bottom issues.	Enforcement and monitoring may be limited owing to a lack of legal basis – mainly based on reputational aspects. The informal nature of regulatory networks is likely to mask unequal power relationships and may strengthen the already powerful regulatory powers. May facilitate exclusion and make monitoring and participation by other officials and non-state actors difficult. Technocratic governance risks supporting the development of a regime with little or no public check on administrative action.
Transnational private regulation	International standardisation can lead to standards and references that are globally accepted by all stakeholders. Enforcement based on contracts and market/reputation pressure is effective in global value chains that extend to countries in which the rule of law is not entirely complied with. Allow heavy reliance on private expertise, which is relevant in markets where the pace of technological change is fast and highly technical information is needed for the definition of implementing measures and technical specifications; and private actors are the most informed parties or the best positioned players to solve a given failure.	Proliferation and fragmentation of private schemes (despite the consolidation under way). The standardisation process tends to be slow and to enshrine existing technical practice. Uncertainty on the performance and on the conditions under which private schemes can constitute a suitable solution to achieve public goals. Lack of accountability mechanisms and under use of better regulation instruments. In some instances, private schemes may fail to achieve comprehensiveness and become clubs of specific interest.
Soft law: guidelines, peer review mechanisms	Flexible tools that can be adapted easily to new and emerging areas / issues.	Compliance and enforcement may be difficult. Countries may feel free to adopt parts of the international instruments and ignore others.
Informal exchange of information	Low-cost mode of IRC, allowing the sharing of practices and to establish common understanding and language on issues. It can help build trust among regulators and provides early warning systems. It fosters regulatory transparency and may help reduce compliance and administrative costs. It is especially effective at bringing regulators together in new fields of regulation where common terminology and approaches need building from the onset.	There is a risk that the co-operation never becomes operational and remains a high-level discussion. The lack of implementation and compliance mechanisms may make this co-operation slow moving and frustrated parties may drop off.

Source: (OECD, 2013[1]).

References

Abbott, K. and D. Snidal (2000), "Hard and soft law in international governance", *International Organization*, Vol. 54/3, pp. 421-456, http://dx.doi.org/10.1162/002081800551280. [4]

Drezner, D. (2008), *All Politics Is Global*, Princeton University Press , New Jersey, https://press.princeton.edu/books/paperback/9780691096421/all-politics-is-global (accessed on 3 June 2021). [3]

Esty, D. and D. Geradin (2000), "Regulatory co-opetition", *Journal of International Economic Law*, Vol. 3/2, pp. 235-255, http://dx.doi.org/10.1093/jiel/3.2.235. [5]

Howse, R. (2012), "Transatlantic regulatory cooperation and the problem of democracy", in Bermann, G., M. Herdegen and P. Lindseth (eds.), *Transatlantic Regulatory Cooperation: Legal Problems and Political Prospects*, Oxford University Press, http://dx.doi.org/10.1093/acprof:oso/9780198298922.003.0027. [9]

Lazer, D. (2001), "Regulatory interdependence and international governance", *Journal of European Public Policy*, Vol. 8/3, pp. 474-492, http://dx.doi.org/10.1080/13501760110056077. [2]

Levy, B. (2016), "Innovations in Globalized Regulation: Opportunities and Challenges", No. 5841, World Bank Policy Research Working Papers, https://ssrn.com/abstract=1953804 (accessed on 3 June 2021). [10]

Meuwese, A. (2009), *EU-U.S. Horizontal Regulatory Cooperation Two global regulatory powers converging on how to assess regulatory impacts?*, Paper for the California-EU Regulatory Cooperation Project Leuven, Brussels, https://ghum.kuleuven.be/ggs/research/biosafety_biodiversity/publications/meuwese_final.pdf . [7]

OECD (2013), *International Regulatory Co-operation: Addressing Global Challenges*, OECD Publishing, Paris, https://dx.doi.org/10.1787/9789264200463-en. [1]

OECD (1994), *Regulatory Co-operation for an Interdependent World*, Public Management Studies, OECD Publishing, Paris, https://dx.doi.org/10.1787/9789264062436-en. [6]

Raustiala, K. (2002), "The Architecture of International Cooperation: Transgovernmental Networks and the Future of International Law", *Virginia Journal of International Law Association*, Vol. 43/1, http://dx.doi.org/10.2139/ssrn.333381. [8]

Annex B. Sectoral studies

Chemical Safety (OECD, 2013[1])

The OECD's Environment, Health and Safety (EHS) programme for chemical safety represents a rare case in which the benefits and costs of international regulatory co-operation have been assessed quantitatively, and demonstrates how this co-operation can support administrative efficiency. This is achieved primarily through the Mutual Recognition of Data (MAD) system, which ensures the acceptance of chemical test results across the OECD and generates estimated annual savings of EUR 309 million. The system is also accessible to countries that adopt comparable testing methods, quality standards and levels of protection beyond the organisation's membership.

Overall, the programme is credited with the development of a common language and classifications, alignment of testing methods, and strong industry support. The MAD system thus illustrates various key functions of international regulatory co-operation in chemical management, including exchanging technical and policy information and administrative burden-sharing. This generates several benefits, such as the reduction of duplication of testing procedures, of non-tariff barriers, and of delays for marketing new products; as well as better management of cross-border risks through enhanced availability of safety data and pooled administrative resources.

The case study highlights a number of challenges to be aware of for the effective pursuit of IRC. For instance, a shift in chemicals production beyond the OECD countries may come with the risk of losing in relevance and legitimacy, the increased complexity and political sensitivity of the technical areas to be addressed once the most consensual topics have been agreed upon, the methodological difficulties of quantifying the benefits of the system, and the uncertainties related to budgetary reliance on member country contributions, particularly in times of budgetary constraints.

Consumer Product Safety (OECD, 2013[1])

The OECD Working Party on Consumer Product Safety illustrates how a joint platform can help countries manage transboundary risks to consumer safety, in a world of rapid and largescale flows of goods and services. The primary objectives of this body include promoting the exchange of information on product safety within and between countries, supporting research on product safety issues, encouraging systematic methods for monitoring and assessing key developments, enabling co-operation between OECD members and non-members on areas of mutual interest, and facilitating harmonisation of product safety requirements and data collection methods.

These processes support regulators and customs authorities in the detection of product safety issues across jurisdictions, foster a consistency in requirements that is conducive to a favourable business environment, and assist consumers in making informed choices and avoiding injury. Challenges arise from legal constraints to cross-border information-sharing, inconsistent approaches to data collection across countries, and garnering sufficient resources to continuously update the information base. The OECD Committee on Consumer Policy aims to address these existing legal constraints to cross-border information sharing, particularly with the draft Implementation Toolkit on Legislative Actions for Consumer Protection Enforcement Co-operation (OECD, Forthcoming[2]).

Model Tax Convention (OECD, 2013[1])

The OECD Model Tax Convention underscores the importance of co-operation for the effective administration of taxation systems and the reduction of unnecessary obstacles to cross-border trade and investment. This instrument enables the co-ordination of internationally-agreed standards for the elimination of double taxation and the prevention of tax evasion, which have formed the basis for some 3 500 bilateral tax treaties. This is supported by the OECD Global Forum on Transparency and Exchange of Information for Tax Purposes, which enables the automatic exchange of tax information across jurisdictions, facilitates the implementation of international tax transparency standards, and carries out monitoring and peer review activities to promote compliance. In addition, the Convention oversees the adoption of common standards, improves the exchange of tax information across jurisdictions, limits regulatory arbitrage, facilitates the interoperability of tax systems, and provides for conflict avoidance and resolution.

These activities contribute to the promotion of shared forms of understanding, comparable approaches, and enhanced co-ordination among tax administrations. However, they are limited in effectiveness by differences in domestic transposition of instruments and institutional set-up.

Competition Law Enforcement (OECD, 2013[3])

The identification and prosecution of anti-competitive practices increasingly requires co-operation among competition authorities, as firms' engagement in these practices spans multiple jurisdictions. The normative foundation for co-operation in this area is the comity principle, whereby countries reciprocally engage in taking each other's vital interests into account when conducting their law enforcement activities. The direct, competition-specific forms of co-operation identified include formal instruments such as national legal provisions and agreements between jurisdictions or competition authorities, as well as informal arrangements such as technical assistance and information exchange. Co-operation between competition authorities is also facilitated through instruments with broader application, including Mutual Legal Assistance Treaties (MLATs), extradition treaties and letters of request. The coverage of these measures can be bilateral, regional or multilateral in nature.

The key benefits emerging from co-operation in competition enforcement include improved effectiveness in providing a remedy for illegal conduct and efficiency by reducing investigation costs and risks of inconsistencies, as well as a reduced need to share confidential information. The core challenges involve prohibitions on the exchange of confidential information, differing definitions of what constitutes confidential information, language barriers, practical difficulties of co-ordination, and resource constraints.

The Canada-US Regulatory Cooperation Council (RCC) (OECD, 2013[3])

Established in 2011, the Canada-US Regulatory Cooperation Council (RCC) arose out of the need for the regulatory infrastructure between these countries to correspond to their level of economic interconnectedness. The RCC is a bilateral arrangement which aims to facilitate regulatory alignment in agriculture and food; transportation; health, personal care products and workplace chemicals; the environment; nanotechnology; and small business ties; with a view to enhancing administrative efficiency and boosting trade and investment. This arrangement enables several forms of co-operation, particularly in the upstream phases of the policy cycle. These include information exchange, research collaboration, common labelling and classifications, mutual recognition, harmonised testing and inspection, shared reference to international standards and standard setting, and joint regulatory development.

The key success factors underpinning the RCC include high-level, sustained commitment across governments; increased levels of protection; strong stakeholder involvement; and a drive to address the systemic constraints barring deeper forms of co-operation. The primary challenges faced involve the lack of robust quantitative evidence for regulatory co-operation – which arises from methodological difficulties – and the federal-only nature of the arrangement.

European Union Energy Regulation (OECD, 2013[3])

Over the past 10-15 years, regulatory co-operation in the European Union's energy sector has become progressively formalised. Through a series of energy reform packages, there has been a movement from softer, informal modes of co-operation towards an increased emphasis on binding commitments and institutionalised oversight. The core objectives underpinning this process in its current form focus on enhancing competitiveness, developing a sustainable energy system, and ensuring security of supply. The primary means through which the European Union seeks to fulfil these objectives include fostering an effective internal market in electricity and gas, setting minimum standards and harmonising technical provisions, overseeing the development of regional energy systems, and enhancing co-operation between national energy regulators. The central actor driving this process is the Agency for the Cooperation of Energy Regulators (ACER), which is supported by an advisory council, deliberative fora, and sectoral industry associations.

There is a comprehensive suite of mechanisms available to support energy co-operation, ranging from information exchange; agenda setting; the formulation of rules, norms and standards; and monitoring and data collection; to supervision and enforcement, dispute resolution and crisis management. In order to fully realise the economic, environmental and security benefits of international regulatory co-operation in the energy sector, several challenges must be addressed. These include entrenched regulatory paths, concerns of regulatory sovereignty, uneven distributions of costs and benefits across countries, institutional differences, technical difficulties, and diverging perceptions of national interests.

The Global Risk Assessment Dialogue (OECD, 2013[4])

The Global Risk Assessment Dialogue demonstrates the role of information exchange and collaborative work in facilitating the development of shared frameworks for understanding, common terminologies and classifications, and the comparability of approaches. This initiative is designed to improve mutual understanding of risk assessments across jurisdictions and foster methodological and substantive consistency in this area. This has occurred through two overarching international conferences on risk assessment, as well as five multilateral working groups in particular thematic spheres. The key actors involved are the scientific community within government agencies and research institutions. The primary activities pursued in this forum concern the development of a common risk assessment terminology, promoting alignment in the communication of uncertainty, fostering reliable and comparable exposure assessments.

The benefits arising from these forms of activity include enhanced transparency, reduced duplication of work, improved knowledge flow, enhanced trust and confidence, and increased scientific integrity. The core issue facing the dialogue is sustaining momentum without high-level political commitment, as well as a lack of institutionalised co-operation and organisational infrastructure.

Prudential Regulation of Banks (OECD, 2013[4])

The global nature of the financial sector and its recent vulnerability to crisis highlights the need for international co-operation in prudential banking regulation and supervision, in order to improve the management of systemic risks and ensure global financial stability. The central actor in this regard is the Basle Committee on Banking Supervision (BCBS), which is supported by the Financial Stability Board

(FSB), the International Accounting Standards Board (IASB), and global committees of securities regulators (IOSCO) and insurance supervisors (IAIS). The three pillars of the BCBS's activity are the co-ordination of responsibilities for cross-border banks, the facilitation of exchange of information on national supervisory arrangements and best practices, and setting minimum standards to foster regulatory harmonisation and contribute to levelling the playing field. The primary instruments mobilised in support of these objectives are standards, which are based on knowledge-sharing and subject to monitoring and data collection.

The benefits identified include the improved management of financial risks, enhanced administrative streamlining and supervisory efficiency, greater commonalities of understanding in relation to financial rules, and better co-ordination among banking authorities. By contrast, the key challenges involve narrow membership and coverage, ongoing difficulties of co-ordination among the relevant bodies, and inconsistency in the implementation of standards.

Transnational Private Regulation (OECD, 2013[4])

The emergence and rise of transnational private regulation is driven by the expansion in cross-border trade, divergences in good governance and rule of law across jurisdictions, rapidly shifting market dynamics, and the increased complexity of a variety of policy domains. The primary actors involved in this process are firms, non-governmental organisations, and epistemic communities. The most frequent type of co-operation pursued is technical and sector-specific, but there has been a recent trend towards more generalised forms. The key instruments developed and implemented in this area are voluntary standards, which regulate behaviour less through formal compliance mechanisms and more through considerations of cost-efficiency, self-interest and reputational aspects. The study highlights the challenges of these schemes, in particular the risk of capture. It calls for their evaluation by public policymakers, which would contribute to their legitimacy and in-depth scrutiny, and encourage policy makers/regulators to identify areas in which they can complement or substitute for public frameworks.

Transboundary Water Management (OECD, 2013[4])

The management of transboundary water resources raises ecological, health and economic challenges, which must be addressed through co-ordinated action among the countries involved. International regulatory co-operation has yielded significant results in this area, exemplified by the negotiation and signing of 295 international water agreements since 1948.

The core instrument governing engagement within and between these actors is the Helsinki Convention, which establishes a minimum framework for agreements between riparian states and the management of transboundary watercourses. This sets out three overarching principles for these parties to observe: the precautionary principle, the polluter-pays principle, and the inter-generational principle. The co-ordinated management of transboundary water resources is further supported by membership of international organisations, facilitating formal regulatory co-operation partnerships between countries through UN regional bodies, establishing dedicated organisations to monitor and implement agreements, the provision of financial support for co-ordination, and the implementation of EU conditionalities.

This contributes to progress in managing cross-border risks and externalities, improved environmental management, increased food and energy production, poverty reduction, transparency and work-sharing across governments, and improved economic integration between co-ordinating states. However, the realisation of these benefits is contingent upon addressing challenges associated with the complexities of managing water resources, uneven distributions of costs and benefits, differences in economic development and governance capacities, and broader political tensions.

International Regulatory Co-operation Arrangements for Air Quality: the Convention on Long-Range Transboundary Air Pollution, the Canada – United States Air Quality Agreement, and Co-operation in North East Asia (Kauffmann and Saffirio, 2020[5])

Air pollution is a classic example of a cross-border policy challenge that offers opportunities for a range of IRC mechanisms. Countries have set up a multiplicity of co-operation efforts to promote air quality and curb transboundary pollution, involving a range of actors and different levels of government. Successful examples include the Canada – United States Air Quality Agreement (Air Quality Agreement) and UNECE's Convention on Long-range Transboundary Air Pollution (CLRTAP). China, Japan and Korea have stepped up their efforts to improve air quality. All countries have unilaterally adopted international environmental standards, collaborate bilaterally on data exchange, technical assistance and capacity-building, and engage in various multilateral environmental programmes, research projects, and joint ministerial meetings. However, a comprehensive regional science-based approach to address transboundary pollution is yet to emerge in North-East Asia. The experience and practices built around the Air Quality Agreement and the CLRTAP provide a useful example to countries keen in establishing similar joint mechanisms.

Trilateral Joint Review – A First for Veterinary Drugs (unpublished)

The joint review and approval of Metacam, a veterinary drug, by the regulatory agencies of Australia, Canada and New Zealand reveals how international regulatory co-operation through the agreement on common language and approaches can contribute to animal health, administrative efficiency and increased trade flows. In practice, this involves an alignment of definitions with regard to residue, harmonised maximum residue limits and a combined regulatory decision. This co-operation arrangement builds on a climate of mutual trust and confidence in the respective regulatory system of the partner countries, which partly stems from their collaboration in two key international fora: the International Cooperation on Harmonisation of Technical Requirements of Veterinary Medicinal Products (VICH) and the Codex Committee on Residues of Veterinary Drugs in Foods (CCRVDF). It is also driven by significant economic and trade incentives, with New Zealand and Australia as leading suppliers of livestock and Canada being a major importer. The simultaneous review of Metacam by the three countries yields important benefits in terms of improved animal health and safety; administrative streamlining and reduced duplication of regulatory efforts; greater international coherence in procedures and decision-making processes; and enhanced trade and consumer choice.

Study of the Equipment Energy Efficiency (E3) Programme between Australia and New Zealand (OECD, 2017[6])

The Equipment Energy Efficiency (E3) Programme is a bilateral arrangement for regulatory co-operation between Australia and New Zealand, which facilitates cost reductions, minimises administrative duplication and enhances environmental management, in particular through the development of joint standards. The central objective of this programme is to establish minimum environmental performance standards and integrated labelling requirements for energy equipment. This is underpinned by the Greenhouse and Energy Minimum Standards (GEMS) Act in concert with the Intergovernmental Agreement (IGA), which spans the various states and territories of Australia as well as New Zealand. The mechanisms of co-operation include a shared registration system and information exchange related to monitoring, verification and enforcement activities. The primary benefits of this form of international regulatory co-operation include economic gains through reduced energy costs, energy efficiency through lowered consumption, enhanced environmental performance through a reduction in greenhouse gas emissions.

Harmonising of Australia's National Road Vehicle Standards with International Standards (unpublished)

The collaborative development and harmonisation of vehicle regulations through the World Forum for Harmonisation of Vehicle Regulations (WP.29) aims to improve road safety, contribute to enhanced environmental performance and energy efficiency, and facilitate trade. The primary benefits of Australia's participation in this forum and adoption of its standards include increased trade, investment, and consumer choice (90% of its vehicles are imported); progress in managing cross-border risks; and administrative efficiency through international burden-sharing in the production of standards. By contrast, challenges arise from diverging priorities and positions among participating countries and national differences in vehicle production profiles and consumption patterns. These are supplemented by the additional costs of monitoring and participating in the relevant international regulatory processes, as well as the length of these processes vis-à-vis their national equivalents.

Trade Costs in Regulatory Co-operation: Findings from Case Studies (OECD, 2017[6])

A focused look into twelve cases of trade-related international regulatory co-operation confirm that trade costs are frequently perceived as significant prior to regulatory co-operation, and conversely, data confirms that IRC can reduce costs and burdens for international trade. This study encompasses a range of sectors (wine, organic products, household appliances, pesticides, vehicles, and seeds), modes of participation, institutional frameworks, levels of commitment, and co-operation mechanisms, demonstrating varying effects of IRC. Overall, among the specific IRC mechanisms examined, the most frequent and pronounced effects were found in mutual equivalence of rules and mutual recognition of conformity assessment procedures, with producers and exporters named as the greatest beneficiaries. Benefits were also reported, although less systematically, for the other mechanisms examined, such as the development of international standards, or the convergence or even harmonisation of rules and conformity assessment procedures, as well as for other stakeholders including importers and consumers. The key factors underpinning the success of these initiatives include the clarification of nomenclature, terminology and concepts; exchange of information regarding regulatory requirements or practices; and the existing of dedicated committees or working groups, particularly in the absence of a formalised framework for co-operation. Respondents also underscored the importance of well-functioning regulatory operational co-ordination; the exchange of research and data across jurisdictions; and supportive political leadership.

References

Kauffmann, C. and C. Saffirio (2020), "Study of International Regulatory Co-operation (IRC) arrangements for air quality: The cases of the Convention on Long-Range Transboundary Air Pollution, the Canada-United States Air Quality Agreement, and co-operation in North East Asia", *OECD Regulatory Policy Working Papers*, No. 12, OECD Publishing, Paris, https://dx.doi.org/10.1787/dc34d5e3-en. [5]

OECD (2017), "Trade Costs in Regulatory Cooperation: Findings from Case Studies", http://www.oecd.org/officialdocuments/publicdisplaydocumentpdf/?cote=tad/tc/wp(2016)17/final&doclanguage=en. [6]

OECD (2013), *International Regulatory Co-operation: Case Studies, Vol. 1: Chemicals, Consumer Products, Tax and Competition*, OECD Publishing, Paris, https://dx.doi.org/10.1787/9789264200487-en. [1]

OECD (2013), *International Regulatory Co-operation: Case Studies, Vol. 2: Canada-US Co-operation, EU Energy Regulation, Risk Assessment and Banking Supervision*, OECD Publishing, Paris, https://dx.doi.org/10.1787/9789264200500-en. [3]

OECD (2013), *International Regulatory Co-operation: Case Studies, Vol. 3: Transnational Private Regulation and Water Management*, OECD Publishing, Paris, https://dx.doi.org/10.1787/9789264200524-en. [4]

OECD (Forthcoming), *Implementation Toolkit on Legislative Actions for Consumer Protection Enforcement Co-operation*. [2]